MEANINGS
OF LIFE

Also by Alex Wright

Why Bother with Theology?

MEANINGS OF LIFE

Alex Wright

DARTON·LONGMAN+TODD

First published in 2005 by
Darton, Longman and Todd Ltd
1 Spencer Court
140–142 Wandsworth High Street
London
SW18 4JJ

© 2005 Alex Wright

ISBN 0 232 52489 0

A catalogue record for this book is available from the British Library.

The author and publisher are grateful to the following for permission to
reproduce copyright material: Gillon Aitken Associates and the Random
House Group Ltd, epigraph from *Birdsong*, by Sebastian Faulks; Cambridge
University Press, epigraph from *The Meanings of Death*, by John Bowker;
and Carcanet Press Ltd, 'The Santa Fe railroad' from *Annunciations*, by
Charles Tomlinson. Every effort has been made to contact the owners of
copyright. Should any material appear herein without permission, the
publisher would be glad to make good the oversight in any future
printings or editions of the work.

Phototypeset by Intype Libra Ltd
Printed and bound in Great Britain by CPI Bath

To my mother and father

'The crisis of our times calls for a truly secular spirituality, and this brave and sensitive book makes an important contribution to the task.'

Richard Holloway, former Bishop of Edinburgh and
Primus of the Scottish Episcopal Church

'Through this beautifully written rendition of a secular spirituality, Alex Wright challenges the need for organised religion. He achieves this through painting a picture of his soul without using the language of formal faith. I have used *Meanings of Life* as a springboard to dialogue between those who identify as Christian and those who have no sense of belonging to a particular religious tradition – a sensitive and difficult conversation yet one which is essential in a post-modern age.'

Jo Ind, author of *Fat is a Spiritual Issue: My Journey* and
Memories of Bliss: God, Sex, and Us

'Moving and evocative, *Meanings of Life* sensitively explores questions at the heart of contemporary spiritual searching. Touching on issues of love, loss and fulfilment, the book offers a tentative yet helpful vision of a meaningful spirituality for our times. Readers, whether they consider themselves religious or not, will have much to gain from it.'

Gordon Lynch, Lecturer in Practical Theology and
Contemporary Culture, University of Birmingham

'This beautifully written and profoundly thoughtful book fills a void created by religious discourses that are overly tethered to the past and blind to the unique circumstances of people living in the early twenty-first century. Alex Wright draws skilfully from his own rich experiences to address that most daunting of all human questions – "What does it all mean". Mining a wealth of human wisdom in contemporary literature, cinema, and religious writings, he offers in these pages a riveting and original spiritual guide to anyone struggling to flourish in the present-day fog of capitalist controlled, narcissistically atomized, and commodity obsessed societies that are wantonly destroying the ecological conditions which are necessary for their very survival.'

Philip Kennedy, Lecturer in Modern Christian Thought,
Worcester College, Oxford

But often, in the world's most crowded streets,
But often, in the din of strife,
There rises an unspeakable desire
After the knowledge of our buried life;
A thirst to spend our fire and restless force
In tracking out our true, original course;
A longing to inquire
Into the mystery of this heart which beats
So wild, so deep in us – to know
Whence our lives come and where they go.

Matthew Arnold, from *The Buried Life*

There could not be a you, and there could not be a universe,
without death, the death of stars, and the death of succeeding
generations of organic life. If you ask, 'Why is death
happening to me (or to anyone)?' the answer is: because the
universe is happening to you; you are an event, a happening,
of the universe; you are a child of the stars, as well as of your
parents, and you could not be a child in any other way.

John Bowker, from *The Meanings of Death*

Hast thou not seen how all in the heavens and in the Earth
uttereth the praise of God? – the very birds as they spread
their wings? Every creature knoweth its prayer
and its praise! And God knoweth what they do.

Qur'an

Stephen climbed the ladder, over the top, into no-man's land.
No hurricane of bullets met him, no tearing metal kiss.

He felt the dry, turned earth beneath his boots as he picked
his way back towards the British lines. A lark was singing in
the unharmed air above him. His body and mind were tired
beyond speech and beyond repair, but nothing could check the
low exultation of his soul.

Sebastian Faulks, from *Birdsong*

Contents

Preface and Acknowledgements

I wrote my last book, *Why Bother with Theology?*, as a sort of manifesto for the kind of theology that I wanted to publish in the context of my previous publishing role. That book attempted to show, in a manner that could hardly be called impartial, that theology still had resonance and relevance in a modern – or postmodern – society, and that there still remained in the Christian tradition much that was of immense value and worth as regards a blueprint for life. My contention was that the tradition offered a powerful antidote to many of the excesses and superficialities of the postmodern zone. At the same time I argued that the tradition was not being heard by those who most had need of its message, and to whom it would probably be of most benefit: those outside, not within, the Church, who remained and remain eagerly concerned – despite their non-churchgoing predispositions – with the meaning and purpose of existence. My argument was that the Church and its theologians, while admittedly subject to the demographics and contingencies of secularisation, had also allowed their own constituencies to drift away through an unwillingness to engage with the real concerns of real people in the real world. 'Theology needs to get a life', as I provocatively put it, 'before telling us how to live ours.'

I little imagined, when I wrote the book, that just a few months later the purpose for which it had been conceived would be as redundant as I was myself. For it was clear that the tenor and message of the book not only fell on hard soil within the hierarchy of my own organisation but that – whatever the rights and wrongs of this – it contributed also to my difficulties within it. Thus, within three months of the book's publication I had left that publisher in precipitate circumstances, and had to face up to the fact that my 'manifesto', such as it was, would never be heard in the way that it was intended to be – that is, in conjunction with a fresh publishing programme that would set the tone for a new kind of liberal publishing in which the distinctive voice of a unique press would be listened to anew by a younger, more open-minded, and more readily questioning, generation of Christians. At the time I was very depressed by this turn of events. My vision for a fresh publishing start was never going to be realised. My book (though in places appreciatively received) was also condemned by sections of the church press who viewed its message as offensive and – this was also clear from the defensiveness and hostility of some of the reactions – frightening.[1] My publishing career seemed to have come off the rails. More pressingly and to the point, I had – after a fairly well-thought-of publishing career, spanning fifteen years – no job and no income.

This setback resulted in a long spell of reflection out of which a new book has emerged. My year-long stint without employment – accompanied by a very pronounced sense of failure and frustration – forced me to ask many acute and sometimes critical questions not only of religious institutions but also of myself and my own motivations, as both religious publisher and private individual, questions which I hope this book will mirror. This is not about exorcising demons, or lamenting that life can be unfair (which would make for self-indulgent writing as well as pretty tedious reading), so much as reflecting on how even moderate adversity can make one more resilient and can lead to valuable insights – especially spiritual insights. Thus, the aim of the book is not to be predominantly polemical, as, broadly speaking, the last one was. My hope is that its tone will be more measured, thereby reflecting the cathartic time through which its author has passed. The intention is to take further some of the critique offered in the first book by reading its questions about purpose and meaning through a grid constructed out of my own personal experience. It is important not to overstate the significance of this experience, and to keep it in perspective: after all, losing one's job and immediate prospects are unlikely to be on a par with coming to terms with the consequences of death or bereavement. However, there's no doubt that my self-confidence was battered and bruised by the perception that my career had been taken from me in a manner that was as unpredictably disruptive as it was emotionally disorienting. By reflecting on the consequences of this, I hope to forge a loose association with a new wave of writing that has lately emerged from some very talented younger theologians and religious writers, who are unabashed about drawing generic lessons from their own lived experience, and who – while themselves critical of the Church, and frustrated by its reluctance to embrace change in the light of postmodernity's challenge – are nevertheless respectful towards the powerful resources which the Christian tradition holds out to Western society and culture.

At the same time, and in other respects, the book will stand very much in the radical, questioning vein which characterised its predecessor. For I propose to show that, in addressing the 'big questions', about life, about death, and about 'meaning' in its broadest sense, Christianity stands as just one – admittedly important and influential – mode of thinking among many others, and that those others have vital things to say to us that can often be as pertinent and helpful as biblical stories, or sermons, or reflections on the parables. It is the 'others', those traditions, whether from religious or secular thought, which stand outside the established Christian thinking of this country, to which I would like to give special attention here, and this will mean the inclusion of poetical and mythological, as well as philosophical and literary, material from a variety of sources and cultures beyond Christianity.

What most concerns me in *Meanings of Life* is that which I tried to characterise in the last book as the numinous and the mysterious: that sense of the larger Spirit moving and energising the universe, the unattainable and unknowable – yet paradoxically knowable – Being whose manifestations may yet (like windchimes in a thunderstorm, or walkers in mist) be perceived indistinctly and in part by those who experience them. Experience is the key heuristic of the book, that lodestone of all human life by which true progress and genuine advancement are measured. The book will therefore move between the specific and the general, as my own particular experiences and considerations of what I would regard as the fundamental concerns of life – love, loss and fulfilment – are conjoined with theoretical reflections on these concerns.

In order to make the book as accessible as possible, I have decided to adopt the format of a 'cycle of meditations', or a series of reflections on loosely connected 'remembrances'. The concept of story was central to my last book, and here I wish to put forward a selection both of personal stories and of stories by others that I hope will lead readers into the material – and the questions raised along the road – in a manner with which they can empathise. Not all the stories will resonate with every reader in the same way or have the same degree of impact. Some of the texts by other writers that I use will be unfamiliar. But I have done my best to provide a representative selection and summaries of them which convey the central truth that the narrative of storytelling (whether within fiction, film or drama) offers a powerful barometer of how a culture measures its own thinking about what, in life, can truly be called authentic.

My aim is to offer thereby something helpful and heartfelt to those many people that I have come across, in the last few years, who are motivated to know more about who and what they are, what they are supposed to be doing here on planet Earth, and about what constitutes, in the twenty-first century, a viable and credible spirituality through which their 'meanings of life' may be known and recognised. Such people may not necessarily think of themselves as conventionally religious, and for whatever reason probably stand outside – or on the fringes of – the churches and the formal worship of other faith traditions (though it would please me greatly if practising Christians, Muslims or Jews, for example, found something worthwhile and digestible here). The book is directed primarily at those who would like to think seriously about ultimate questions of meaning and value, from whatever perspective – secular or religious –

and who are prepared to come at those questions with an open and enquiring mind. Such readers may well already have sought for 'answers' in the burgeoning field of self-help books or popular psychology. While some of this literature is illuminating, much of it, I find, is not; so my aim is to provide an alternative view – a text that adopts a committed stance on transcendence, and which critiques the failings and self-regard of the West even while it does its best to stimulate and point in some fresh directions.

It will be clear to the reader from the start that this is not intended to be a scholarly book, so I hope that he or she will make allowances for the brevity with which complex issues are sometimes treated, and for the generalisations and oversimplifications which must inevitably follow from the limitations of the format – as well as from the author's own limitations, of course. It is a deliberately impressionistic, unsystematic and personal book, and its consequent imperfections may perhaps be offset by a hoped-for readability and accessibility (qualities which, regrettably, are often lacking in religious books of any kind). I must first warmly thank my editor at DLT, Brendan Walsh, for his unwavering support and implicit confidence in my abilities, which have been a significant source of encouragement through both good times and bad. I would also like to express my appreciation to Iradj Bagherzade and Jonathan McDonnell, my senior colleagues at I. B. Tauris, for their own support, and for their vision of a meaningful religious studies list that is neither defined nor contained by faith confessionalism. Various others have at different periods, and often unbeknown to them, set me thinking about some of the ideas which, however imperfectly expressed, have made their way into the book: and in this connection I must mention Madeleine Ladell, Ronnie Cloke, Andrew and Luisa Livingston, Rima Morrell, Gela Roberts, David Lorimer, Alasdair Clayre, Jenny Jones, Ben Okafor, Alison Lawson, Laurence Hallam and Alison Webster. Jo Ind, Richard Holloway, Philip Kennedy and Gordon Lynch generously read the draft of the manuscript and offered much support as well as many penetrating insights. Over the course of planning and writing the book, and thinking about loss (to which a chapter is devoted), I encountered loss in a personal way when an author to whom I was particularly close, Colin Gunton, died suddenly and unexpectedly. I am uncertain whether Colin would have found any merit in what is printed here, but for my part I have certainly derived much inspiration from his friendship and loyalty, which I miss a good deal. It will be obvious from the text how much I owe to another of my authors, John Bowker, whom it has been my privilege to publish on several occasions. I hope that John will forgive the inordinate attention I give to his ideas here, though that prominence is perhaps indicative of how much they have influenced me. I have dedicated the book to my parents, who in their different ways have given me rich material to draw on over the years. Finally, to my partner Alison (who with tolerance and understanding has put up with my disappearances while I wrote the book, and has supported me throughout), I owe more than acknowledgements such as these can properly convey.

Introduction: What Does It All Mean?

To attempt to write a book called *Meanings of Life* may seem at best a dubious undertaking. The issues may be evergreen, but any author who tries to wrestle them to the ground knows from the start that they have preoccupied the greatest of thinkers since recorded history began. At worst, the project may look presumptuous and ill advised. It may be that I am deluded in thinking that I can offer anything more – or more meaningful! – to the vast corpus of writing that already exists on the subject. However, in my defence I could point to the continuing hunger for answers to the most fundamental of questions (Who am I? Where am I going? How long have I got?[1]) as being in itself indicative that the issues remain worth engaging with, and from a variety of different perspectives. And the very fact that the questions are so often raised, directly or indirectly, in contemporary culture, indicates that there is ongoing mileage in asking why this should be so, and what possibilities exist for these questions' resolution.[2] As to my own credentials for tackling the subject, I can point only to my continuing interest in metaphysical issues (despite having my fingers burned, on more than one occasion, through involvement with institutionalised religion!) and my professional reliance, as a religious publisher, on their exploration and explication. In other words, I have a vested interest in discussing 'ultimate questions', and in discovering where the questions, as well as the answers – however tentative – appear to be leading.

This book, then, is about meaning. Not so much meaning as an abstract principle, but rather meaning in our lives as an experienced and lived reality. Note that the title is quite clear that what is being addressed is not one sort of meaning, but *meanings*, in the plural. I would never wish to claim that life can be reduced to one sort or set of meanings at the expense of others. Neither is there an assumption that what are being explored here are *the* meanings of life. My meanings are not definitive meanings, since I believe that meaning and value are to be found in a multiplicity of different ways and different forms. Furthermore, in a context of what is often called postmodernity, where old stories (such as the Christian story) so often fail to transport us, the idea that one narrative has an authenticity foreign to all the other stories seems both anachronistic and in my view distastefully imperialistic. It is also seriously out of kilter with many people's increasingly lived out experience of twenty-first-century diversity and plurality. In a society where our neighbours are as likely to be Muslims or Sikhs as they are Anglicans or Catholics, it is imperative that one becomes sensitive and mature about the value of absolutes. And the perils of religious fundamentalism, which is on the increase worldwide, indicate just how dangerous such absolutes may be. There are many meanings to life, just as there are multiple levels of complexity and ambiguity. What this book hopes to do is to offer a sort of road map, to help guide people along the road they are already heading. What on earth does it all *mean*? is in many ways the defining appeal of human existence. It is the *ur*-question that has preoccupied philosophers from Plato to Camus, from Nietzsche to Derrida. Most of us at one time or another are confronted with the crisis of our own apparent purposelessness. It is what Jean-Paul Sartre called *angst*, that sensibility of acute anxiety which tells us that we are mortal, that our lives are mean and small, and that we must die. *Timor mortis conturbat me*, as the medieval poet William Dunbar put it: the fear of death disquiets me. Or not so much death, as the meaninglessness which it encompasses. As Prospero chillingly philosophises: 'We are such stuff as dreams are made on, and our little life is rounded with a sleep.' For Albert Camus, the stark fact of mortality gave rise to his overriding philosophical question: if we're already, at birth, on the road to oblivion, why not hasten the inevitable by bringing the pointlessness of life to an end by one's own hand?[3] At least suicide could be understood to represent the proactive dignity of taking charge of one's existence and its consequences, rather than feebly submitting to dissolution.

In his novel *October Ferry to Gabriola* the author Malcolm Lowry recognises the absurdity of life, when he writes about the bathetic conditions under which life's key decisions – the decisions which ought to give life its meaning and dignity – are actually arrived at:

> Perhaps it was at such moments, with hangovers in movies – as in pubs, hamburger stalls, lavatories on ferryboats, in addled but profound prayer, in drunken dreams themselves – that the real decisions that determined one's life were often made, that lay behind its decisive actions, at moments when the will, confronted with its own headlong disease, and powerless to save, yet believes in grace.[4]

Lowry was prone to a jaundiced view of human nature, more especially evident in his depiction of the louche and drunken British Consul to Mexico, Geoffrey Firmin, in his masterpiece *Under the Volcano*. Yet it is his use of religious language – 'prayer', 'grace', 'save' – in the passage quoted above, a conceptuality underlying his entire fictional oeuvre, that ameliorates his tendency towards misanthropy and despair. For theological notions figure strongly in Lowry's work, as they do in the creative processes of many of those whose activities and philosophies have so often attracted ecclesiastical opprobrium or censure.

In *Why Bother with Theology?* I tried to show that there is much in Western secular culture that earnestly seeks engagement with some of the most important questions that there are, but which remains unacknowledged or unappreciated by the Church. I concentrated particularly, in this regard, on examples from contemporary fiction and film. I suggested that the hierarchies of the Church – especially the Church of England – could learn much from the richness of secular life and culture, both intrinsically, and with a view to 'speaking' to their congregations in ways that

might make sense to a generation for whom biblical and liturgi-
cal givens were meaningless. Since writing that earlier book my
own feelings about the value of 'theology', at least as this seems
to be understood by its current generation of practitioners, have
shifted. I am less certain now that the 'beards and sandals'
Christian theology that now seems to predominate in many university theological departments (I exempt those secular departments of religious studies whose ethos has much more to do
with the social sciences than the church) has anything left to say
that has not been said before a hundred times over, probably
more interestingly. And it is my perception (garnered from
fifteen – progressively tortuous – years of theological conference
attendance) that this is a theology that offers demonstrably
diminishing returns, both because by its own nature or choice it
is conservative and stuck in the past, and because fewer and
fewer people accept its underlying assumptions and presupposi-
tions. My progressive realisation has been that the religious
interests that make sense to *me*, and which have power and
meaning for *me*, are not those shared (at least outwardly) by the
theologians whose books I have for so long been publishing. It
has been a Road to Damascus event, for sure, but in reverse. The
scales may indeed have fallen from my eyes, but not with a view
towards renewed churchy vistas. The road is not towards
Jerusalem, but into the liberating highlands where the air is
purer, the scenery more varied. The sun may have gone down in
the West, but here on the mountaintop the stars emerge with
reassuring lustre.

This is not to say that Christian theology doesn't have a place
in critiquing the excesses of contemporary secular cupidity and
avarice. The Christian tradition rightly places great emphasis on
the importance of community and of consideration towards
others, an area where many contemporary spiritualities, with
their strong orientation towards discovery of the self, and apparent lack of social or cosmological interest, often appear to be
deficient. The tensions that exist between individualism and
commonality, and of how people reconcile their own needs with
the wider demands of the communities which shape them, are
issues and challenges which this book hopes to explore. So when
Rowan Williams inveighs against the unfettered greed, lust and

selfishness of the culture of celebrity parodied to brilliant effect in TV shows like *Footballers' Wives*, we can all acknowledge the good sense (as well as the sheer, holy *goodness*) of what he says.[5] The Anglican Communion is fortunate indeed to have as its leader a man of such obvious gifts and ability, even though nasty and increasingly powerful elements within it would appear to have every intention of getting shot of him at the earliest available opportunity.[6] It's just that, for me, what the Church and its theologians have to say (given that – with some notable exceptions – their pronouncements are so markedly and depressingly self-referential) seems to have less and less relevance. And I am representative of the large majority, as all the figures for church attendance bear out. Certainly we can recognise the truth in the charge that Western culture is in many respects degenerate; that our children, fed on a diet of unremitting materialism, undiluted by any kind of moderating code that recognises worth and value in things unrelated to acquisitiveness, are in danger of becoming the most self-indulged and socially alienated generation in history.[7] So the question, then, is what to do when the old Christian ecclesiastical structures totter and fall. When the establishment can no longer be said to represent the vibrant and demotic country that contemporary Britain – at least in its urban centres – has become, what is there that can replace it? Do we turn to the various manifestations of New Age religion? Or do we simply dismiss religion altogether as the clapped out superstition of an earlier, pre-modern mentality?

As Linda Woodhead and Paul Heelas indicate in the findings of their Kendal project, people would appear to be turning to alternative forms of religious expression in a manner that bears out my earlier claim that religious feeling is far from dead in (seemingly) secular Britain. They predict that interest in and participation in associational 'holistic' spiritualities (including everything from yoga to pagan rites) is set to overtake church-based (or 'congregational') religiosity within forty years.[8] The valuable empirical research undertaken by Woodhead and Heelas underscores the anecdotal evidence available from every town's supermarket grapevine or post office notice board: that there is a remarkable and burgeoning interest in 'spirituality' at the expense of institutionalised Christianity, which is regarded –

especially by younger generations – as unattractively authoritar-
ian and liturgically forbidding. What is not so clear, either from
the Kendal project data or from general anecdote or observation,
is of what such 'spirituality' really consists. Is this a search for
one's inner self? Or for a connection with a transcendent force or
being? Or both? Is this about finding meaning in the divine or in
the true nature of human personhood? One of the problems
currently faced by sociologists of religion is the difficulty of
defining exactly, or even approximately, what 'spirituality' is.[9]
There are disagreements about whether it signifies belief in the
metaphysical or whether it denotes, rather, an existential interest
in the identification of the true nature of the human soul (which
I use here as a shorthand for the totality of human being, often
referred to by New Age writers as 'mind, body, spirit'). Yet
despite the ambiguities and complexities, the broad patterns are
clear: 'spirituality', understood as a plethora of socio-religious
phenomena which operate outside the boundaries of church
jurisdiction or legitimation, is likely soon to supplant church-
going in its claim upon the contemporary religious imagination.

The contemporary postmodern condition – that condition in
which new spiritualities have taken root – has led to what has
often been characterised as the breakdown of grand or 'meta'-
narratives.[10] The old certainties no longer hold good. In the news-
papers we read daily of the breakdown of relationships, of the
disintegration of family life, and of the rootlessness of the young.
The culturally predominant conservative press in particular ful-
minates about the lack of clearly defined 'values' and principles
by which society may be ordered, and – like many bastions of the
establishment – nostalgically lyricises a vision of an England that
is slipping away because of the damaging inroads made by a
variety of bogeymen and women: from asylum-seekers supposedly sponging off the state, to young British Muslims corrupted
by imported imams preaching militant Islamic fundamentalism.[11] In contrast, the minority left- (or centre left-) leaning press
is usually able to recognise the many positives that are associated with ethnic diversity and immigration, as well as the benefits
that may result from the breakdown of outdated assumptions
that are fundamentally elitist, colonialist and xenophobic.
Nevertheless, wider Western dependency on technological

development at the expense of larger frames of meaning – and on materialism at the expense of a mature, holistic sensibility which cherishes our connectedness with the planet and its limited resources – have led to impending ecological disaster and our betrayal of the global custodianship that is the unique inheritance of the human race. The unfettered capitalist drive deleteriously affects all our relationships: with the planetary ecosystem which we pollute, despoil and defoliate; with the animals and plants we drive to extinction; with the people we starve and deprive of clean water; and with the conflicts we precipitate with our neighbours to protect our own interests and commodities. The result is a profoundly atomistic view of human nature, where 'progress' is measured in terms of self-advancement and individual profit rather than by a responsible, generous outlook that includes the purview and interests of others rather than concentrating on the immediate gratification of ourselves.

It is no accident that the upsurge of Islamist terrorism worldwide coincides with a widespread sense of injustice and disenfranchisement by the Islamic communities, because self-interested and exclusive actions inevitably have damaging and anti-social consequences. The destruction of the twin towers and attack on the Pentagon on 9/11, and more recently the commuter train bombings in Madrid, while in themselves horrible and morally reprehensible, appear to have resulted from the deep anger felt towards the West by Muslims who think that Western governments operate according to geopolitical double standards. The hypocrisy of the latter is seen to be manifested in the self-serving ways that the Western nations – especially, but not exclusively, the United States – conceptualise the Israel–Palestine crisis (where the Palestinians are so often reduced to the part of bit-players); or in the moral hypocrisy that they bring to bear in propping up a corrupt Saudi regime and condemning the Baathist Iraq of Saddam Hussein (having armed and supported that same Saddam for the best part of a decade); or else in these governments' rapacious economic exploitation of the natural resources available to Islamic countries (resulting in wealth for the few at the expense of grinding poverty for the many).[12]

While the exploitative capitalism that constitutes the defining socio-economic mode of our world has profoundly damaging ramifications at the macro level of international relations (and directly plays into the hands of the fundamentalists, whether Protestant, Catholic or Islamic), as well as of our increasingly precarious relationship with the environment, the materialism that is part and parcel of Western economics also seriously and adversely affects our daily relationships with our own peers. Our society is by turns self-regarding, vain, shallow and posturing. We are increasingly obsessed by the banality of celebrity lifestyles, seemingly as a distraction from the panic and emptiness which so many of us feel inside. Young people can still be idealistic and want to put the world to rights, and yet many of them appear to be selfish, narcissistic and detrimentally obsessed by commodification. The determinative and all-encompassing confusion of the postmodern context is well recognised by Madeleine Bunting, who writes of the rising mental illness consequent upon the constant and disruptive change associated with the implacable imperatives of the market:

> It's not that people have gone soft so much as they are
> profoundly disoriented by the ceaseless continuity of change.
> Experience becomes utterly random and meaningless. You
> were doing really well in your job but you still got fired; you
> thought your relationship was strong but your partner has
> fallen out of love with you. Appalling images of suffering in
> the world are interrupted by advertisements for car insurance:
> barbarism and banality, cheek by jowl. What lies behind the
> weight of escalating emotional distress is that awful struggle
> to make meaning, that instinct that our lives should have a
> narrative and a purpose and should make some sense.[13]

She continues:

> Whereas previous generations had a very strong grasp of the
> meaning of their lives (whatever the catastrophes which befell
> them), of their own identity and where they belonged, we are
> living out of Marx's prediction that 'all that is solid melts out
> of air, all that is holy is profaned.' Meaning inspires resilience:
> if you have some explanation for what happens, it gives
> strength. That's what past generations drew comfort from. It is

the sheer meaninglessness of the chaotic instability of our experiences which exposes us to despair. We have no answer to the 'Why me?' We have no account for the suffering which is the inevitable lot of human beings – death, disease, betrayal, frustration – other than to employ desperate strategies to avoid them.[14]

In a context where very little seems to 'make sense', in a world where fracture and fragmentedness are themselves encountered as just one further set of nihilistic encounters alongside the processes of ceaseless self-gratification and consumption, how do we live in any way that seems to have integrity, coherence and dignified self-possession? In previous days the churches might have provided the glue with which our wayward selves could be stuck together, thus offering the metaphysical and conceptual framework upon which people could build the structures through which they and their lives might develop and be sustained. No longer. Despite the global success of sectarian Protestant Christianity, and the resilience of Christian religiosity in the USA (where religion is so thoroughly bound up with nationalistic interests that it has taken on a peculiarly introspective and parochial, as well as partisan, hue), there seems little doubt that Christianity in the UK and Western Europe is in serious decline. The demographics of secularisation, as well as the deficiencies of the churches themselves in responding to secularity (phenomena which I have documented elsewhere[15]), have led to a widespread loss of Christian influence, prestige and credibility. And as for the places where Christianity is on the march, there is an alarming tendency here to resort to evangelisation in the worst – fundamentalist – sense, and try to impose on others the Christian perspective on life as this is understood by its followers. Stephen Bates, for one, skilfully charts a determined and sinister minority of conservative evangelicals who are wrestling for control of the Church of England in his recent book *A Church at War*.[16] But such a phenomenon is especially noticeable in the USA, where, as Will Hutton remarks in a recent *Observer* article, 'reformist social and political movements are undermined by its sheer continental scale, along with a deeply felt, faith-based individualism.'[17] For those North American

Christians who want to convert others to their cause, human purpose expresses itself in the mirror-image of Islamic fundamentalism, and in its own way is just as unpleasant and damaging as the Islamist version: it desires to dominate others through adherence to a single 'explanation' of meaning by way of ideological exclusivism and fanaticism.

As Hutton points out, there has always been a tension in religion between the moral message (what do we do, and how do we do it?) and the ontological belief (what is the point of all this?) – in other words, between doctrine and ethics – that it tends to promote in parallel (and, as he rightly says, the different world religions have a remarkably similar moral compass). For Hutton it is the 'why' not the 'how' question that has contributed to our present geopolitical ills, at least in the religious sphere, because while 'everybody seeks a purpose; to make a difference; to be part of something; to belong', it is the pursuit of their faith that is the abiding purpose for religious people, whereas for the secular citizen 'that purpose can be building a great society, a great work of art, a great business or a great family, against which religious values may or may not be an important backdrop.'[18] For Hutton, who confesses that he remains loyal ('just') to the Christian camp, what is needed is a rediscovery of a belief that purpose 'is best attempted in a secular guise underpinned by universal values', and that 'religion is a moral code to live by, rather than a purpose in its own right that gives believers the right to deny rationality and humanity.'[19] Yet Hutton is still able to talk about the importance to him of the 'transcendent capacity of love to produce understanding',[20] a theologically resonant statement which suggests that he may still be motivated, in his understandings of 'meaning', by more than simply humanistic idealism or secular moralism.

One of the most interesting younger writers on religion and culture, Gordon Lynch, has written recently about the importance of prioritising lived experience over abstract concepts in making sense of 'the value of life'. Lynch, closely following the existential theology of Paul Tillich, points to what he calls a 'God above God', the ultimate reality 'that lies beyond any concept or label we can create, of which we may be fleetingly aware at different points in our lives'.[21] Such reality, the ground of human being and of everything else, is to be detected in places that to conventionally religious people might seem surprising. As Lynch says:

> Helpful 'religion' in contemporary culture may take a much wider variety of forms from more overtly 'spiritual' activities such as meditation or yoga, through outdoor activities such as walking, travel to remote parts of the world and playing sport, through to other forms of popular culture such as dance . . . Now it is clearly easy enough to depict all of these simply as leisure activities, or perhaps to characterise them as expressions of hedonism in contemporary culture and to say that people engage in them simply because they find them pleasurable. But if, even if just very rarely, we gain a sense of connection with a greater reality or a sense of indescribable joy or deep peace of mind through these physical activities then they could be seen as contributing to a search for meaning that goes beyond mere hedonism.[22]

The variety of processes which Lynch describes of reaching for attunement with the ultimate force behind life are I think closely related to what I described in my last book as our search for the indefinably, unknowably mysterious. Whether it be in the riotously bacchanalian immolation of the Man at the Burning Man festival in Nevada; or the Wiccan rites of Beltane; or druidic chanting at Stonehenge at the summer solstice; or even in the primordial joy of contemporary dance – there is often to be found here a serious, sustained seeking after the life-centring, life-giving essence of all that we and our planet are. This seeking is nothing more nor less than a quest for the meanings behind existence. Christians are dismissive of such popular manifestations of religiosity, and in my experience their hostility seems to be based as much on a bewilderment that they do not command the same sort of fascination and following as, increasingly, do practitioners of the New Age, as it is upon their conviction that they are the only ones with access to the right kind of Truth (with a capital T). What I want to explore further in this book is the notion that there are legitimate and helpful forms of 'secular spirituality', or spiritualities that are located, buried, and

manifested in areas of secular life and culture, which can help us
to make sense of the confusion and disorientatedness of life in
the twenty-first century. I am not going to investigate in depth
the various different forms of spirituality, whether in paganism
or Wicca, or even in yogic or other meditative practices, since
this has been done elsewhere and by those better qualified than
me to undertake such investigation.[23] Neither am I going to try to
define 'spirituality', since, as I've implied, this is a business
fraught with disagreement and uncertainty. What I am going to
try to do is explore through my own experience those locales of
'meaning' which in themselves, or in relation to other significant
locations of spiritual value, help to make sense of the business of
living in the miasma and – as it frequently seems – opacity of the
postmodern zone.

I am particularly concerned here with the importance of storytelling, with the idea, outlined most helpfully by the theologian
Sallie McFague,[24] that stories are part of the fabric of ourselves:
that they not only faciliate communication and understanding
with each other but that they define who we are in relation to
the divine. The business of living is, after all, the continuous
business of telling stories: stories of love, of anger, of betrayal, of
forgiveness, of grief and of redemption. These stories course
through our lives, like leaves on the water, like water over stone:
they ebb and flow, a stormflecked tide, against the shores of
all our waking days and visonary nights. The stories we tell
conjure up visions of something greater than ourselves, of
the true being beyond the shadows on the wall of Plato's
cave,[25] of the reality behind the dream. Storytelling has always
provided people with more than just entertainment, and even in
the absence of one grand Story (as one might call the Christian
story) there remain many others that can help us to see where we
are headed and where our paths might end. Jenny Diski recognises this well, when she writes that every single human being
experiences their own story as unique, and 'worth the telling
because it had happened to them and not to someone else'.[26]And
yet, as Diski says, after reflecting on her many conversations
with travellers on journeys she has made by train round the
USA:

It was their personal existence that made their story
remarkable . . . The same story told by another person was not
the same story. It did not matter how many times people had
carelessly opened doors and caused an untroubled life to have
to confront death, how many times the goodness in life had
been squeezed dry by an addiction to alcohol, how often a
damaged brain had caused an innocent to be sent away from
society, to each person it happened to, it was the first time it
had happened to them, their one and only story and each of
them told it, to themselves and others, with a sense of wonder
that they had such a story, that they had a story at all.[27]

The stories I am going to tell are part of my story, the narrative
that is uniquely me, but in sharing them here they become, in
their reading, part of your story, and perhaps also cast a ray of
light onto a yet bigger, more transcendent, story. My hope is that
my stories, with the reflections and remembrances that accom-
pany them, may in a small way have something to say about
wider questions of meaning and value that is worthwhile and, as
Diski puts it, 'worth the telling'.

CHAPTER 1

Self and World

First, heaven and earth, and ocean's watery plains,
The moon's bright orb and the titanic stars,
A breath within them nurtures.

Virgil

My first recollection: there it is – a huge, painted flower on the wall beside my cot. It is dark red – a rose – and looms over me like an angry cloud, filling my world.

The late sixties. My brother and I, aged 2 and 4, are playing by the shore of Frensham Pond, a mile-square stretch of water in Surrey. Determindedly, Ian is digging in the sand with a spoon, his furrowed toddler's face an alternating checkerboard of feeling, as fierce concentration strives for dominance over the contented expression of an explorer who is now opening up the frontier. As for me, I soon tire of the game with the spoon, and am distracted by the attention of another child who has shyly approached our little group to talk to us. Our father is soon watching the three of us – Ian, me and the other little boy – playing 'catch' in the long grass at the edge of the pond. Dad looks happy as he paddles away from the beach and the sunlight flashes like silver fish below his rolled-up trouser legs in the water.

Later still. The eighties. My father and brother and I are walking the length of Danebury Ring, an iron-age hill fort close to our home in Winchester. There is a susurration in the tree tops, and the leaves of the beeches and elms are rustling, a whispering refrain which the long timothy grasses take up in apparent empathy. It is summer. A bloated, crimson sun sinks leisurely below the Western hills like a deflating balloon. The residual works of the Belgae, the ancient tribe of the Hampshire Downs, mark the abandoned ridges, scuffed and eroded by the tramp of our ancestors' careless descendants. We are picnicking in a spot hidden from the path, shaded by conifers, that is all our own. The peanut-butter sandwiches and the cheese and pickle sandwiches, the apples, the squash and the chocolate biscuits have all been shared around. The earthwork is draped in an eerie twilight expectancy that sucks out conversation. The sun has vanished at last, and the sky is combusting, irradiated by strips of pink and red cloud, shot through with black and dark grey – a flamboyant patchwork which fills the stratosphere from nadir to zenith.

Fast forward again. My parents have separated, pending divorce. I have just said goodbye to my mother, who has gone to live in a house in Suffolk that – with appropriate symbolism – stands alone in a cornfield. My father is driving her there. My brother is out. The car is gone, and suddenly the deserted house is full of memories, razor-sharp, overpowering, that knock the breath out of me like a fighter's punch. I have been self-contained, seemingly in control, up to this point, but now something in me gives way, crumbles and withers, like a piece of scorched and quickly disassembling paper in fire. I stumble to my knees by the steps of the back door, and weep at last, incapable of controlling the tears which drop onto the floor that Mum brushed for the final time that morning.

Crying again. My first girlfriend – my first **proper** *girlfriend – and I have parted. It's over. Done with. 'The love-boat's smashed against the reefs of day-to-day existence' – Vladimir Mayakovsky. And on the shoals of inexperience and naïveté. Speaking to my father on the phone from Cambridge, suddenly I am crying, and I can't stop, and Dad doesn't know what to say or do. Can't catch my breath, can't cope. It's over. Finished. First love gone for good.*

The north Norfolk coast. Late summer. Besides the muddy banks of Blakeney Sound the sailing boats are resting in an ordered line, their pennants catching the wind like the circling gulls overhead, their

rigging tinkling in an accolade of tiny bells. Brightly coloured sails –
yellows, turquoises, crimsons – are visible along the sandbanks and
river flats, as the craft in the estuary lurch and bob between tidal
surges. A warmth-giving westerly breeze, infused with the scent of the
sea and fragrant with the pollen of hedgerow flowers, gently brushes
my cheeks and hair. I stand on the river bank, and listen to the sighing
current and chiming boats, and lift my face to the heat of the sun, and
I think: I am happy here, this is me, this is my life, my unique existence
which is part of something more. My feet are in you, now, here, on the
turning earth, looking up at a star.

What is it that makes us who we are? Not just the spinning memories that shine or cut to the quick, but the predispositions, the
preferences, the unique personalities that define us in relation to
ourselves and to one another. But what is 'the self'? A molecular
bundle of bone and blood predetermined to live and die by a
genetic code? Or a soul, a spirit that exists independently of body
and flesh, that is distinctively 'other' than our corporeality,
which is related to, yet is somehow different from, mind and
intellect? And does the 'self' find its way to God, at the moment
of physical dissolution – as Christianity and Islam would propose – or is it endlessly reborn, in the cycle of *samsara*, as the
Hindu *Mahabharata* would suggest? Or is all reality, even the self,
illusory, and the residue of karmic consequence, as Buddhism
outlines? The literature on these questions is vast and unresolved. Rather than address the unaddressable (or at least the
addressable only in encyclopedic depth), what concerns me here
is not so much *what* we are as the *meaning* of what we are – and
as I see it that is a question that can really only be framed reli-
giously; or to put it another way, in terms of a transcendent point
of reference.

    Despite all the suffering and pain in this world, the injustice
and the cruelty, despite the death camps and genocide and
Rwandas and Cambodias – despite all the terrors and tortures
that human beings have visited on each other – I have always
accepted that there is a meaning at the heart of things, a fundamental sentience independent of creation itself which though
invisible to our senses remains emotionally and psychologically
discernible. Such discernment is difficult to describe or quantify:

is it 'faith'? Is it 'belief'? Is it a generalised, diffused 'feeling'? It is certainly not based on the conviction of biblical revelation or of inviolable Christian 'truth'. I suppose at bottom I accept – despite the protestations of Richard Dawkins – William Paley's argument from design,[1] that the visible evidence of the world and its manifestations of life suggest the workings of a discrete and compassionate intelligence, without which the created order would not be animated or exist. Beyond this acceptance, like many people nowadays I am not sure which religious or spiritual road to take, since religion clearly is determined culturally and, while I still am drawn to Christianity for what I suspect are predominantly social and historical reasons, my Christian heritage is fundamentally an accident of birth and geographical location. It doubtless makes excellent sense to be a Hindu in Uttar Pradesh, just as it is entirely understandable to go to confession if one is born into Catholicism. My aversion to statements of absolute truth, which invariably have been divisive and costly, in human history – and which are profoundly at odds with postmodernism – is also bound up with a sense that the transcendent cannot be delimited in one location rather than another. To do so is to try to grapple with shadows, and there is in any case a mystery at the heart of things which is resistant to assertions of religious 'fact'.

A discernment of the mysterious Other is not to mimimise the sufferings of those who are afflicted, or the very great evils that are part and parcel of life on this planet, whether visited on others via the genocidal predilections of a tyrant or dictator, or through the smallest cruelty of one child hurting or bullying another. And indeed 'God' often seems very far away, undetectable to sense or belief or prayer. But there are still moments when – like Sam Gamgee in Tolkien's story, and confronted on all sides by horror – I can look beyond the immediate landscape, blasted and ruined as it looks, and express the hope that high above all this there is a star resistant to contamination.[2] This is not to say that such belief is not subject to incessant doubt and questioning. It would indeed be tough, in the face of the abominations which are part of the fabric of life, not to wonder if human degradation is not all that there is in the universe, and that where we lie there do we rot. It is hard, very hard, to hold

on to the fact of transcendent beauty or value when confronted
by the obscenity of the murder of children and comparable acts
– often inexplicable acts – of depravity.[3] Nor is it to say that such
belief is not, and should not be, hard won, if it can be won at all.
There is a meaning to life in adversity and struggle which has an
integrity and a credibility about it that are not necessarily present in soft living or in always taking the easy path. Ursula Le
Guin, as so often, puts it well in her novel *The Dispossessed*, when
her character Shevek reflects on the nature of pain:

> Suffering is the condition on which we live. And when it
> comes you know it. You know it as the truth. Of course it's
> right to cure diseases, to prevent hunger and injustice, as the
> social organism does. But no society can change the nature of
> existence. We can't prevent suffering. This pain and that pain,
> yes, but not Pain. A society can only relieve social suffering –
> unnecessary suffering. The rest remains, the root, the reality.
> All of us here are going to know grief; if we live for fifty years,
> we'll have known pain for fifty years. And in the end we'll die.
> That's the condition we're born on. I'm afraid of life! There are
> times I – I am very frightened. Any happiness seems trivial.
> And yet, I wonder if it isn't all a misunderstanding – this
> grasping after happiness, this fear of pain . . . If instead of
> fearing it and running from it, one could . . . get through it, go
> beyond it. There is something beyond it . . . I don't know how
> to say it. But I believe that the reality, the truth which I
> recognize in suffering as I don't in comfort and happiness –
> that the reality of pain is not pain. If you can get through it. If
> you can endure it all the way.[4]

Life's central certainty is that we are all going to suffer, since
this is the condition on which we are born. Whether it be in the
gulags or the death camps, the indignity and poverty of the
shanties or inner cities, the heartbreak of rejection or the death
of a loved one – from the highest to the lowest, from the earth-
shattering to the mundane, each human being is going to be put
through the flames, to a greater or lesser degree, of affliction.
'And in the end we'll die.' There is no escaping the fact of mortality, of the final finish: the folding away of the chess board once

all the moves have ended. The prolific Montreal-based theologian Charles Davis wrote a book entitled *Soft Bodies in A Hard World*, which well encapsulates the human condition, the inroads that this pitiless world progressively makes into our weak flesh, so that finally worn out, or destroyed by some other happenstance, our corporeality crumbles to nothingness.[5] And the hardest condition of all is indeed finitude, that nothing lasts – of ourselves there is no final legacy, only the traces that we leave behind. And yet . . . and yet, there seems to be some essential, indefinable human quality, some intrinsic dignity of self, to be found in such transience and in the capacity to bear stoically what life may throw at us, for good or ill, and even if we suffer terribly in the business of staying the course. Perhaps this is the essence of being human, the 'reality' as Le Guin's character Shevek puts it in the above passage. For as Shevek remarks elsewhere in her novel,

> If you can see a thing whole it seems that it's always beautiful. Planets, lives . . . But close up, a world is all dirt and rocks. And day to day, life's a hard job, you get tired, you lose the pattern. You need distance – interval. The way to see how beautiful the earth is is to see it as the moon. The way to see how beautiful life is is from the vantage point of death. All you have to do to see life whole is to see it as mortal. I'll die, you'll die; how could we love each other otherwise? The sun's going to burn out, what else keeps it shining?[6]

Le Guin understands perhaps better than any other 'popular' writer that I know that life is tough, criss-crossed with ambivalences, hard decisions and disappointments. And ultimately, it is finite. The compassion and humanity that she brings to her writing are testimony to her deep understanding of the facts of life. And her wisdom seems to me to be rather more potent and credible than the sanctimoniousness and complacency which church-people sometimes bring to the question of suffering, as if affliction is somehow to be accepted without question as the necessary corollary and obverse to the sufferings of Christ. No – the process of questioning, objecting, arguing with the spurious authority of establishment Christianity is essential if we are to remain true to ourselves as intelligent, rational creatures made in the image of God. But the question still remains: who or what is this 'we' that suffer and die? As I've already suggested, the solutions to this conundrum have preoccupied the greatest of thinkers since history began.[7] The nature of personhood is deep and complex, and there are wide cultural as well as philosophical differences in understanding who and what we are. But like the Anglican philosopher of religion Vernon White, in his recent book *Identity*, I find it plausible that there is an essential unity to human being. In other words, 'however we are brought into being, and whatever changes we may experience, we do not then become a sequence of different persons, nor do we become something other than persons.'[8] And like White I also accept that what matters is to 'live and act on this basis, in relation to ourselves and others'.[9] As White says, without any sense of an enduring 'I' in the future 'in any sense as the same person as I now am', this erodes one's sense of responsibility 'for any action with long-term consequences'.[10] Thus, if we are to think of people, as the philosopher Derek Parfit does, merely as bundles of provisional and unstable dispositions, which somewhat echoes the Buddhist view, one is forced into the position of accepting, as White puts it, that

> I will not own either 'my' past or future. It fails to provide any basis for valuing other people in relation to their past and future, except in so far as they currently value it for themselves. This has a strangely flattening effect in human relations – and a potentially chilling one if we reduce the significance of the very young or elderly to their present personhood, unrelated to the wider narrative of their lives.[11]

There is a markedly pragmatic slant to the best contemporary Christian theology – of which, with its erudite philosophical content, White's book is a notably strong example – and a practically orientated intent which we ought to take as a yardstick. What matters in conceptualising human identity is not so much how our physical, chemical and emotional dispositions seem to us, as how we behave towards others. But perhaps it might be better to say that we are as we do: how we live appropriately and responsibly in the world *itself* defines who we are as human beings. Having said that, one of the most powerful indications of our ongoing continuity, which gives a solid foundation to our relationships with others, is memory, a mark of human person-hood (as well as a valuable tool in understanding 'meaning') that I want to explore in further chapters. Vernon White recognises as much with the emphasis that he places on storytelling, and on the recounting of tales that give substance to human identity while at the same time bridging the ages: 'Story-telling, with its profound implication for the unitary person, spans the centuries and crosses cultures.'[12]

And yet the spectres of death and suffering still loom large. How do we navigate those dark seas, or make sense of the apparently senseless? Another theologian, John Bowker, wrote a whole book addressing the meanings of death, as he understood them, in the various religious traditions of the world, and to my mind it is still the best account that remains of the religious apprehension of mortality. (It is also one of the best religious books I know, well deserving the Collins Religious Book Award that it won in 1993.)[13] For Bowker, the key to both religious and scientific explanations of death lies in what he refers to (in Charles Williams' phrase) as 'the way of exchange', of life giving way to life via the process of entropy: everywhere in the universe there is a need for energy from somewhere else in order to create life, and such energy is only available through the dissolution of other forms of life. This means, put bluntly, that 'you cannot have life without death: but where you do have death, there you have the possibility of life.'[14] Bowker's theology of sacrifice, of life giving way to life so that more life can be secured, leads him to imply that the ultimate meaning of life is found in the consummate sacrifice: that of Jesus on the cross. This will not be convincing to everybody, since it necessitates an acceptance of the broad swathe of Christian doctrine regarding the incarnation – though it has to be said that there is an attractively sceptical and internally coherent character to Bowker's theologising that eludes many less intelligent and open-minded Christians.[15]

Yet Bowker acknowledges that countless people have made brave sacrifices, throughout human history, for the sake of others,[16] and this leads him to ask what end and purpose such

self-sacrifice might serve. The law of entropy – of the reorganisa-
tion and reattribution of molecular life – is one very fundamental reason why sacrifice is necessary, for sure. The mutations in
the evolutionary process, which enable more complex organisms
progressively to evolve, are only achievable via the sacrifice of
one form of life for another. Life is only possible on the condition
of death. But this bald scientific assertion doesn't go very far
towards explaining the presence in the world of love, sensation,
the appreciation of beauty and virtue, if they all come to nought.
As Bowker says, it may be the negentropic organisation of
energy which, like children on the beach, has created us as a sort
of human sandcastle to resist the surge of the oncoming tide. Yet
in the end 'the tide will prevail, and the outward forms of all this,
and of all that we see, and of all we love, will be carried into a
different shape and outcome, far beyond our competence: the
tide will be smooth once more.'[17]

For Bowker it is in the glory of our relationships with others
that the fullest religious significance is achieved, since in relationships of grace and love, we already realise that the physical
fact of death is transcended, 'at least in a preliminary way'.[18] In
the business of living in community, in dialogue and engagement with other human beings, we are able to reach 'levels of
experience which reach through particular death, and which are
far beyond those of the stones or the trees or the lilies in all their
glory'.[19] I think this is the right approach, in the religious quest
for 'meanings to life'. Although Bowker implies that there is a
continuation of particularities of life even as they disassemble
for the benefit of other lives, and for the sake of the general life
process ('in the context of a universe of this kind, the resurrection
is not especially surprising'[20]), it is not the sort of fate that befalls
us after death and dissolution which most preoccupies him, but
– as with Vernon White – what happens to us while we are here
in relationship with others. It is the *here and now* – the discernible
small miracles of grace and love to be found in the everyday –
which is important, and this emphasis on praxis has all sorts of
implications for the religious notion of how we should live our
lives well and responsibly.

Perhaps, by this understanding, the meanings of life can only
properly be understood according to how we live our individual

lives in relationship with our neighbours. The self, however we conceptualise it, cannot be comprehended in isolation from our fellows. The kind of atomism which we see in Western society, and which so antagonises radical Muslims, is a kind of cosmic alienation, where people no longer understand their wider 'meaning' and purpose in terms of good neighbourliness, generosity and love. The capitalist drive, unhindered by rejoinders regarding compassion and social sensitivity, has become hegemonic and corrosive. For example, we are fascinated by a succession of apparently beatific (but actually utterly banal) celebrities because adulation of them seems to confer some reflected sense of worth or of 'being special': feelings which we crave. But when, entirely predictably, they cannot provide us with the sustenance we need, we take great delight in destroying the idols at whose designer-shod feet we have worshipped so fawningly. Love has become self-love. Value has become self-obsession. Tulsi Das (1532–1623) wrote: 'Show love to all creatures, and thou wilt be happy; for when thou lovest all things, thou lovest the Lord, for he is all in all.' While for Plato, 'the desire and pursuit of the whole is called love.' This is the lesson that we need to learn again, in the West. Our society's loss of a sense of the transcendent – the beneficent wholeness that is found in the centre of things – of the kind that was mediated through the churches and Christian faith, and that is now sought fitfully and sporadically in other places, is reflected in our loss of a broader fellowship with each other. I would like to argue for the recovery of a sort of religious pantheism, where 'meaning' is understood in the sacred and holy interrelationship of people, places and of all creation. Meaning of this kind can be profoundly redemptive and healing, and is often explored by secular writers. For instance, at one point in his splendid novel *Birdsong*, Sebastian Faulks writes of the power that a sense of connectedness with the 'sentient landscape' (to use a phrase of Alan Garner's[21]) exercises over a recovering British officer, Stephen Wraysford, who in 1917 is on a short leave in England from the carnage and misery of the Picardy trenches. There is nothing especially Christian about Stephen's sense of religious transportation, but his is an experience nevertheless of powerful and authentic spirituality:

Stephen felt himself overtaken by a climactic surge of feeling.
It frightened him because he thought it would have some
physical issue, in spasm or bleeding or death. Then he saw
that what he felt was not an assault but a passionate affinity. It
was for the rough field running down to the trees and for the
path going back into the village where he could see the tower
of the church: these and the forgiving distance of the sky were
not separate, but part of one creation, and he too, still by any
sane judgement a young man by the repeated tiny pulsing of
his blood, was one with them. He looked up and saw the sky
as it would be trailed with stars under darkness, the crawling
nebulae and smudged lights of infinite distance: these were
not different worlds, it seemed now clear to him, but bound
through the mind of creation to the shredded white clouds, the
unbreathed air of May, to the soil that lay beneath the damp
grass at his feet. He held tightly onto the stile and laid his
head on his arms, in some residual fear that the force of
binding love he felt would sweep him from the earth. He
wanted to stretch out his arms and enfold in them the fields,
the sky, the elms with their sounding birds; he wanted to hold
them with their unending forgiveness of a father to his
prodigal, errant but beloved son. Isabelle and the cruel dead of
the war, his lost mother, his friend Weir: nothing was immoral
or beyond redemption, all could be brought together,
understood in the long perspective of forgiveness. As he clung
to the wood he wanted to be forgiven also for all he had done;
he longed for the unity of the world's creation to melt his sins
and anger, because his soul was joined to it. His body shook
with the passion of the love that had found him, from which
he had been exiled in the blood and the flesh of long killing.[22]

This is the sort of spirituality which increasingly preoccupies
a variety of contemporary secular writers,[23] whether they be
novelists like Faulks, 'nature' poets like Charles Tomlinson, or
academic psychologists like Brian Bates. (I'll come to Bates and
Tomlinson in a moment.) My sense is that on several fronts
this spirituality would not necessarily go under the designation
'religious', or 'Christian'; yet there is a serious interest being
shown, knowingly or unknowingly, in questions of 'meaning'

and 'purpose' which are bound up with a keen sense of the mysterious, unknowable Other that is manifested all around human beings, and yet transcends their natural faculties. Such a transcendent sensibility is not only part of the landscape in a passive way, but can effect active transformation as well, since people's ideas of how the landscape impacts on their moral and emotional compass can completely reorientate their perception both of themselves and of the world they inhabit. Thus, for Stephen Wraysford, 'nothing is beyond redemption . . . understood in the long perspective' – that is the holistic sense of all things coming together in a kind of transcendent wholeness – 'of forgiveness'. Such a perspective can come to us unexpectedly, just as it did to me standing on the bank of the Blakeney estuary several summers ago; or it can come regularly, in the cumulative sense of 'passionate affinity' with creation that came to me many times walking Danebury Ring near Winchester. In both cases, however, there is a clear sense that the ordinary has crossed over into the extraordinary: that a particular landscape or event or happening at the borderlands of existence – where life becomes painful, or notable, or 'rememberable' – has become imbued with special power and meaning.

In the work of Charles Tomlinson, who before his retirement was Professor of Poetry at Bristol University, one often gets a sense of this 'coming together' of the mundane and the sacred. The most ordinary observation can become the catalyst for an almost mystical appreciation of the context of the poet's subject. Thus, in his short poem 'The Santa Fe railroad', which is a quintessential expression of his capacity powerfully to convey the relationship between the human and natural worlds, Tomlinson manages to evoke a landscape and mood that are seemingly representative of a purer and more transcendent state of existence. Such existence, moreover, points beyond things as they are in themselves to something 'else', a mysterious other that lies beyond the observable fact of a railroad whistle and which encapsulates the essence of a whole geography, with all its accompanying resonance of character and history:

> *The tri-toned whistle of the night-train*
> *Starts up a blues that goes no further*

Than this one repeated phrase, and yet it goes
Far enough. The desert has no need
To declare itself by fanfare. It is itself indeed
As you and I might be only in Eden.
And so the three tones – flattened on the final note –
Float out over so much of space
There is no more to say except: these notes
Express enough of possibility and of sadness, too,
To tell the extent and loneliness of the continent.
Is that not so? – I ask Adelicia, who replies
When you catch the trainsounds here, it's going to rain.[24]

The work of an earlier poet, from another culture – Govind
Singh – similarly recognised the transformative power of landscape, and detected there the presence of the divine, which was
both part of and distinct from earthly existence. In the following
short prayer-poem the tension between immanence and transcendence is perfectly expressed:

God is in the water, God is in the dry land, God is in the heart.
God is in the forest, God is in the mountain, God is in the cave.
God is in the earth, God is in heaven . . .
Thou art in the tree, thou art in its leaves,
Thou art in the earth, thou art in its firmament.[25]

The success of Peter Jackson's film trilogy of *The Lord of the
Rings* has inspired the psychologist Brian Bates to try to uncover
the 'real Middle-earth', and Bates is a writer who in doing so
might be seen to have much in common with both Tomlinson
and Govind Singh, as well as with Sebastian Faulks, since he is
fascinated with the connections between people and the environment which sustains them, and which can powerfully effect
change. In the post-Roman era of England, which was characterised by successive waves of Anglo-Saxon and Norse migra-
tion, Bates shows how different to that of today's Englishmen
and women was the inhabitants' view of their world – the world
of the actual 'Middle-earth' – and in particular of the natural
world. Our mindset today, a legacy of both Christian and
Enlightenment thinking, tends towards domination and mastery

of the landscape. But the people who lived on these islands before us had a much more nuanced and complex relationship with their surroundings. As Bates brilliantly shows, 'for our ancestors, the imagination was the doorway from the everyday to the Otherworld. And there was a constant flowing of the imagination into the material world. The sense of reality in Middle-earth was more a sense of realities, in the plural.'[26] While for us landscapes have by and large become a matter of aesthetic appreciation, or the source of exploitable raw materials, for our ancestors in the early Middle Ages they were much more than that, being alive throughout with spiritual presence. Our ancestors thus viewed nature 'not only as an objective world, external to themselves, but as also reaching internally, with magical powers and imbued with the full richness of their imagination. Features of nature had many layers of meaning, levels of significance, allusions and messages. The forest was alive with the chatter of another world.'[27]

As Bates indicates, trees were an especially potent means of connection between the human and the transcendent, since they represented 'the very essence of spiritual reality in cosmology',[28] while the very word 'tree' – *treow* – also meant 'trust' or 'truth' in Anglo-Saxon. For this reason, 'trees were even thought to provide witness for the most serious of contracts between people. Sacred vows, such as marriages or pledges, were carried out in the presence of these spirits of nature – rather like a pre-Christian ceremony equivalent to swearing on a Bible.'[29] Yet as Bates shows, the church authorities unsurprisingly objected to such unlicensed ritual: 'One of their proscriptions admonished "No one shall go to trees, or wells, or stones . . . or anywhere else except to God's church, and there make vows or release himself from them."'[30] Similarly water, for the Norse and Anglo-Saxon mindset, flowed with more than just lifegiving or physical significance:

Every spring, every woodland brook, every river in glen or valley, even lakes were imbued with the presense of a spirit. It was not the wide-eyed marvelling at the appearance of a spring which directed such sacred thoughts, but rather the sense of connection with a realm more encompassing,

transcending and deeply imaginative. Waters were, for the
people of Middle-earth, flowing from the very source of life.[31]

Bates thinks postmodern people need to get back into touch
with that part of themselves that they have lost, in order to
reconnect with the earth-centred spiritual realities of the ancestors of these islands. And that missing part of their identity is
composed of a connectedness between landscape, memory and
storytelling:

> For thousands of years people have been enthralled by
> essentially the same adventures, whether told by Stone-Age
> storytellers or cyber-age producers of feature-films. The stories
> are so compelling because they emanate from dreams that
> animate the most ancient depths of our consciousness. Like all
> mythology, they are stories which capture the essential spirit of
> our lives, from all cultures. Often they came from the visions
> and dreams of people identified as wizards, sorcerors,
> shamans and seers – those in the community whose
> imaginations were believed to receive material from the spirit
> world. We are most disconnected, fragmented, exposed, frail,
> when we are separated from the deep dream – the story of the
> earth's mind, the rhythm of its beating heart. It is the
> landscape of our deep imagination. And when we read about
> the real Middle-earth, we feel reconnected with ourselves.[32]

The sort of landscape that this writer describes is of significant
concern to the practitioners of the many earth-based spiritualities to be found at centres of New Age spiritual activity like
Glastonbury, where there is evidence of a considerable interest in
the imagination and its relationship to the natural world. At
Glastonbury there are many followers of goddess mythology
and of pagan figures like the Green Man,[33] and participants also
in the spiritual power of place, particularly with regard to the
continuing resonance of the interlocking Grail and Arthurian
myths; and on the summit of Glastonbury Tor at sunset, so startlingly crowned by the tower of the ruined church of St Michael,
one feels keenly the enduring presence of these legends about
the so-called 'Isle of Avalon'.[34]

The Glastonbury mythology begins with St Joseph of Arimathaea and a band of missionaries, who – despatched from Palestine by Philip the apostle – carried the Christian faith to Britain in AD 63. Joseph brought with him the Holy Grail, the cup supposedly used at the Last Supper in which he had caught drops of Christ's blood at the scene of the crucifixion. Making landfall in Cornwall, the group made their way towards Glastonbury. Arriving at nearby Wearyall Hill, Joseph thrust his hawthorn staff into the earth and at once it burst into bloom. He settled on the site of present-day Glastonbury's abbey ruins, and built there the first Christian church to be constructed in Britain. Joseph is popularly supposed to have buried the Grail some-where on Chalice Hill in Glastonbury, and this legend connects with that of Arthur and his knights (lately re-explored in Romano-British guise by Antoine Fuqua's film *King Arthur*),[35] who long searched for the Grail to restore bounty to a famine- and drought-ravaged countryside. In time Glastonbury came to be identified with Avalon, the mythical island of apples to which Arthur was carried by three black-robed queens after the battle of Camlann[36] and his final showdown with the would-be usurper, Mordred, who in some versions of the legend was his nephew, and in others the son he sired by his half-sister Morgause (who is often conflated – as in John Boorman's film *Excalibur* – with Arthur's other sister, Morgan-le-Fay). This asso-ciation of Glastonbury with Arthur appeared to be corroborated when in 1191, after a revelatory vision, a monk of the abbey dis-covered a coffin professing to be that of Arthur and Guinevere. On the coffin was found the inscription 'Here lies the famous King Arthur buried in the Island of Avalon'. When it was opened, the coffin revealed skeletons which seemingly were indeed those of the king and queen, who were positively iden-tified by means of Guinevere's golden locks, still lustrous and miraculously preserved. These tresses then crumbled to dust when handled by the monk. Though this 'discovery' is dismissed by some contemporary historians and archaeologists as a ploy on the abbey's part to gain power and influence by association, there is nonetheless a powerful tradition in English – and espe-cially West Country – folklore which maintains that one day the Grail will be rediscovered, at which point a number of ancient prophecies will be fulfilled, including one which speaks of the resurrection of Arthur. Glastonbury will then emerge as the epicentre of the nation's spiritual and cultural rebirth.

Whatever credence one gives to the veracity of these legends and their 'meaning', I was struck on a recent visit to Glastonbury by the fact that the gradual interweaving and symbiosis of Christian and pagan mythologies has resulted in something extraordinarily evocative and compelling, so that the Grail legend, and the legend of the Glastonbury Thorn (as well as the Arthurian myths) are framed by a complementary interest in wicker men and Wiccan symbols and runes. The cross-fertilisation of Christian and pagan is perhaps best epitomised in the form of the Chalice Well, situated in a valley between the Tor and Chalice Hill (as we have seen, reputedly the site of the Holy Grail's burial place), which is Glastonbury's most remarkable shrine to the earth goddess as well as a sacred spring with reputed healing qualities linked to St Joseph and the Grail. The site is a setting for both Christian and pagan ceremonies (such as celebration of the summer solstice), and is therefore a remarkable advertisement for pantheistic and inclusivist religious activity, where different beliefs can coexist – and indeed thrive off one another's powerful mythologies – successfully and to mutual benefit. This effective coexistence of pagan and Christian is echoed by the design of the well covering, whose symbol of the *vesica piscis*, or two interconnecting circles, designed by Frederick Bligh Bond,[37] is representative of the merging worlds of matter and spirit. In Glastonbury's shops Celtic crosses and Wiccan runes are displayed side by side, and may both be purchased as pendants, together with every other conceivable manifestation of New Age commerce. Many of the artefacts on sale admittedly are tourist tack (of the kind that one tends to find in any holy site – from Walsingham to Santiago di Compostella – which, besides being venerated for its sacred significance, has also become a magnet to tourists and daytrippers). But if one looks beyond the gaudy beads and the witches' cauldrons, one finds in many of the earnest inhabitants of the town an underlying and serious interest in metaphysical questions which are related to issues of environmentalism and responsible ecological custodianship. New Age adherents walk the streets alongside

holy men from India, Tibet and elsewhere, who are drawn to
Avalon by virtue of its reputation in their own countries as a site
of extraordinary holy power. On nearby Dundon Hill, a neo-
lithic hill fort, which is situated close to a supposed axis of sacred
energy – a trackway of holy 'stations' along the spine of western
England[38] – one also feels that one is close to the deep springs of
being, or of a greater reality than ourselves which may yet have
a personal impact on our lives. Given Dundon's distinctive
'essence', it is perhaps not surprising that in 1929 the artist and
mystic Kathryn Maltwood identified the site as being that of the
head of the Gemini figure in her Glastonbury Zodiac, an astrological pattern formed by natural and ancient artificial features
of the local topography.[39] Ringed by dark elms and ancient oak
trees, the earthwork at dusk seems haunted yet by the residual
spirit of its former Durotrige inhabitants, who have left this
indelible mark on the landscape of western England, which
looks out north-west towards the dark bulk of the Polden Hills,
westwards towards Sedgemoor across the Somerset Levels, and
northwards towards Glastonbury Tor, unmistakable and inspiring for miles around. To survey such a landscape, and appreciate
its latent power, is perhaps to experience what Paul Tillich called
'the ground of our being', that existential reality framing our personal existence which, as Gordon Lynch describes it,

> Gives us what Tillich describes as 'the courage to be'. This
> courage is the ability to acknowledge that our lives are limited,
> that the universe can seem a random and meaningless place,
> and that our lives will inevitably come to an end one day. Yet –
> as Tillich puts it – we can demonstrate faith and courage if we
> can still live in constructive and creative ways in spite of these
> realities. Such faith is not something that we can generate
> purely within ourselves, however, but arises out of an
> awareness of that which is greater than ourselves and our
> individual lives.[40]

To venerate the world around us, to love it as we love ourselves, and to detect within it a spiritual energy that has personal significance for the way we relate to it and to one another
– all of this has profound implications for the way we live our

lives. For then the world itself becomes holy and impressed with sacred power; and as part of the world and of the created order, we too are holy and should treat our bodies and minds with an appropriate reverence and respect. The exploitation of the natural world, just as our exploitation of each other, becomes a sacrilegious as well as just an immoral act. In this regard, we in the West have much to learn still from indigenous peoples like the aboriginal peoples of Australia, for whom the concept of 'ownership' of the land (at least in the sense that we understand ownership, as being separate from identity), or indeed of any commodity apart from its essential usefulness to the tribe, would be as nonsensical as it was ridiculous.[41] The aboriginal belief is that the earth was traversed in 'dreamtime', by ancestral beings who exercised supernatural power and energy. These beings were not people, but a combination of human, plant, animal and of elemental components such as fire, earth and water. The geography of the land was formed by the travels of its dream-time inhabitants, and, as Robyn Davidson explains in her book *Tracks*, their energies remained on earth in important sites or landmarks where significant or special events had taken place: 'Contemporary man [sic] receives part of these energies through a complex association with a duty towards these places.' As Davidson indicates, these are 'what anthopologists call totems – the identification of individuals with particular species of animals and plants and other natural phenomena'.[42] Thus particular rocks, trees and other natural features 'are imbued with enormous religious significance for the people who own a particular area of country and have the knowledge of ceremonies and stories for that country'.[43] The rituals that the elders hand down to the tribe are the means by which the potency of the dreamtime is made manifest in the present day, and they relate directly to the sacred sites which, rather than being owned by clan members, own them.

The results of such a world view, in effecting a whole reorientation of the self and of our day-to-day perception of reality, can be seen in the apprehension of transcendent landscape which Davidson began to detect, while making a courageous journey by camel through the 'dead heart' of the world's oldest continent, in her responses to the Australian outback, which are experienced as a kind of rebirth:

> All around me was magnificence. Light, power, space and sun. And I was walking into it. I was going to let it make me or break me. A great weight lifted off my back. I felt like dancing and calling to the great spirit. Mountains pulled and pushed, wind roared down chasms. I followed eagles suspended from cloud horizons. I wanted to fly in the unlimited blue of the morning. I was seeing it all as if for the first time, all fresh and bathed in the effulgence of light and joy, as if a smoke had cleared, or my eyes been peeled, so that I wanted to shout to the vastness, 'I love you. I love you, sky, bird, wind, precipice, space sun desert desert desert.'[44]

Like Robyn Davidson in her travel memoir, we need to begin to see ourselves as extensions of the world for which we have responsibility – which we do not 'own' to exploit, but which we have on trust; which has been given to us as a gift, and through which we perceive – sometimes tantalisingly, like glimpses of the sea from the winding coastal road – that sense of something altogether larger than us, the transcendent and animating power of the universe which is yet inextricably bound up with our individual lives and destinies. What this thing is may be impossible to name or define. Religious traditions of every colour and complexion have tried to describe it, and yet the greatest thinkers of religion know that whatever they theologise can never come close to pinning it down.[45] Yet it exists in us, and through us, and to know it in our relationships with one another, and in our use of what Brian Bates calls our 'deep imagination', is to have a sense of where its echoes may be heard. Thus, when we talk about 'meaning', we need to keep in mind above all the context of our lives and selves: this finite world, inhabited by the fragile intelligences and sensibilities of the people whose care it is, and through whom its latent powers will be known 'according to their works'. All too easily we can misuse and pervert our custodianship to twisted and misguided ends, as the past and current ills of the world distressingly bear out. But to love our neighbours and our planet as we love ourselves, so that we make

of our lives a 'living sacrifice', in the sense that John Bowker
understands it, is to come close to hearing the rushing Spirit of
the universe, at whose spring the parched can drink, and to
understand, as Ursula Le Guin so artfully reminds us, that this,
and no other, is the Kingdom of life:

> This is your immortality. Look at the hills, the mortal hills.
> They do not endure forever. The hills with the living grass on
> them, and the streams of water running. In all the world, in all
> the worlds, in all the immensity of time, there is no other like
> each of those streams, rising cold out of the earth where no eye
> sees it, running through the sunlight and darkness to the sea.
> Deep are the springs of being, deeper than life, than death.[46]

To have a glimpse of the mystery of being is to understand the
power, as Le Guin puts it so well, that exists in every blade 'of
the wind-bowed grass, every shadow, every stone'. So when
someone 'stands in a cherished place for the last time before a
voyage without return, he sees it all whole, and real, and dear, as
he has never seen it before and never will see it again'.[47]

CHAPTER 2

Loss

Take this kiss upon the brow!
And, in parting from you now,
This much let me avow –
You are not wrong, who deem
That my days have been a dream;
Yet if hope has flown away
In a night, or in a day,
In a vision, or in none,
Is it therefore the less gone?
All that we see or seem
Is but a dream within a dream.

I stand amid the roar
Of a surf-tormented shore,
And I hold within my hands
Grains of the golden sand –
How few! Yet how they creep
Through my fingers to the deep,
While I weep – while I weep!
O God! can I not grasp
Them with a tighter clasp?
O God! Can I not save one
From the pitiless wave?
Is all that we see or seem
But a dream within a dream?

Edgar Allan Poe, *'Is All that We See or*
Seem but a Dream within a Dream?'

August 2002. I am standing on top of the Worcestershire Beacon, the highest point of the Malvern Hills. Ahead of me a huge sky stretches out, immeasurable, a brilliant azure, as clouds dance away to the horizon and the border with Wales, beyond which the peaks of the Black Mountains are just perceptible. All around me there is sunlight, dappling the pre-Cambrian rocks of the fells a speckled orange-blue. I must be able to see for twenty miles in every direction, and the view is magnificent. Across the valley to the east looms the brooding bulk of Bredon Hill, A. E. Housman's poetic inspiration, and still inspiring, where the water tower that squats on its Iron Age summit is silhouetted against the skyline. I can visualise now, from across the valley, Bredon's dark woods and siren false summits, which tantalise and mislead the walker, as mist envelops the landscape like a sinister smoke. I have hiked there many times this summer, and recall clumps of gorse and thistle looming out of a silent whiteness, while herds of startled deer jump up and vanish into the shadowy, waiting trees. White, silent, empty. It counterpoints the disorientation I feel in my own soul, that sweaty, ghoulish and mysterious hillscape, where one cannot find one's bearings, and whose mist descends so suddenly, soaking my skin in warm and clammy moisture. Yet here today, on the Malverns, buoyed up by light and luminosity, I feel connected to different elements than those of their sultry counterpart: air and fire, not water and dank earth. I can forget for a while my troubles on Bredon's curdled slopes, and be transported on the Beacon by the sense that time and space have run together in a moment of infinite presence, of immanence and transcendence conjoined – a moment when sky and rock signal change and transformation.

Another time, it seems another age. En route from LA to San Francisco the plane cruises on the slipstream of perception. Ahead of me stretches not just the shimmering horizon, redolent with possibility, but the prospect too of a full portfolio of trips to Berkeley and Stanford Universities, where soon I will talk about important books with some of America's leading theologians. Far below me the San Francisco Bay takes on the qualities of a translucent pool of indigo ink, strafed by periodic flashes of surf and sunlight in a late November morning in the Fall. I am secure in my career, I am 25 years old, I am working for the oldest and supposedly one of the most prestigious publishers in the world. Life has no markers to hold me back, no boundaries to demarcate impossible from possible. All is light, lightness, and a bright and exhilarating ride towards a destination that lures me, youthful and unencumbered as I am, like a holy grail that must be sought and won. A quest for excitement and fulfilment will turn into an exploration of myself, as I learn how to live with the loss of what once I valued above all else.

When, years later, I was jobless and had time on my hands, I was thrown back on my own resources. Those with busy careers tend to think in only a single dimension. Life is defined by humdrum questions, taken for granted in their immutability. But without the daily rhythms of distraction, or the continuity of that engagement with others which is the oxygen of office activity, where then does one look for an air supply? Many of us know ourselves, or think that we do, through the work that we perform. But when deprived of the piles of paperwork, the flow of manuscripts, the contact with authors and the energising exchange of ideas, which were the stuff of the profession that I had, I was forced instead to turn inwards. What does this loss mean? What do I want from my life? These questions now seem banal, written down. But then, thoroughly disoriented and miserable, I felt them race round and round in my head, imprinting themselves in letters of fire that left scars. Suddenly existence – everybody's, and my own – opened out in vistas unknown: disturbing, horizonless, unpredictable.

Unable to get work, I went to the gym. As I pounded the running machine, hours sped into days which flowed into months. My feet became hammers, repeatedly beating the ground in frustration. Then I lifted weights, cursing my sense of insecurity and disempowerment as sweat poured off my body in rivulets. Time dragged with the confused and shambling stagger of a drunk. Always the same routine, the same faces in the locker room, and the same backbeat of sinuous writhing by MTV's televised dancers. Their manic flutterings seem as frantic as butterflies' wings in a killing jar. They're a voyeur's specimen of faux femmes fatales, served up for our consumption by monitors that flicker, blink and are suspended from the ceiling in rows of roving, implacable eyes. I don't know who I am in this place. It feels empty: soulless and pointless. The women on the multiscreens gyrate and grind in a commodified simulation of provocation, while those who watch work out. With hard glances, emptied of meaning, the pouting faces look down

*and jeer. Do they taunt me, or themselves, or both? And on and on the
dance beat races, like the pulse of a skydiver in freefall.*

*In misery we come to know ourselves. 'The more that sorrow carves
into our being, the more joy we can contain' – Kahlil Gibran. Gibran
was right. In experiencing adversity, I am wiser, more resilient, more
appreciative of a bright day, or of the sheer sensory glory of walking in
summer rain, than I was before. Any joy can be taken away at any time.
But it is precisely that knowledge which infuses all our moments of
happiness with their fleeting, and so poignantly human, texture of
intensity.*

*Remarkably, the church, for once, is full. The congregants look at the
vicar in expectation and hope. Is there to be a miracle today, a rebirth?
No, it seems we have come merely to mourn and remember. My grandfather's coffin lies beside the pulpit, in front of the quire. It looks peace-
ful there, and at rest. He was an extraordinarily vigorous man, but at
last, at 90, his vigour is gone, as has his life. It seems incredible, literally unbelievable, that he is dead, still more so that he died physically
diminished and in pain. None of us can take it in. The vicar tells us
about him, and there is a hush as the stories begin to turn back time.
Like weak tea, the insipid greyish light of a damp autumn afternoon
leaks through the church windows into that sombre space where life is
done. There follow readings by family members which try to offer some
adequate sense of who and what my grandfather was. At last it is my
turn to approach the lectern. My voice at first faltering, my determination to do him justice finally allows me to speak clearly the words for
which I'm grasping. He was a man who loved and lived on the countryside, a woodsman, working class, and largely uneducated, though
wise in the ways of nature. I wish to convey no mystery, no untruths,
in what I say, in order to dress Grandfather up in richer clothing than
he wore. I want only to convey some sense that he is, and will always
be, part of what he loved: the sandy chalk soil of the South Downs, the
wind in the branches, the birds on the air. As the words weave their
spell, I glance across at the coffin with the gathering sense that my
grandfather can actually hear the sentences I'm speaking. The glowing
eyes of the mourners fasten on mine, and the words that fall into that
opened silence magically work their way into the place between life and
death, so that we all begin to see a vision of Granddad as he was, and*

is: whole, and complete. 'Do not stand at my grave and weep, I am not
there, I do not sleep. I am a thousand winds that blow, I am the diamond
glints on snow. Do not stand at my grave and cry. I am not there. I did
not die.'

Loss is the inevitable and unavoidable consequence of living.
'All on this earth shall pass: your mother, youth; a wife betrays,
friends leave you suddenly', as Alexander Blok so succinctly
expressed it. Bereavement, grief, disappointment, death – these
are facets to life that all of us must encounter and must wrestle
with in our own ways. Because, although these phenomena are
universal, the experience that each of us has of them is singular,
unrepeatable and unique. No one can measure the depth or
boundaries of an individual grief. For instance, there are no
marks for whether one death is 'better' – or, for that matter,
'worse' – in its effects and consequences, than another. The final-
ity of each death makes its own impact, precisely because death
is so final; there is no definitive moment when the messiness
of life's meanderings will be resolved, no comeback, and quite
possibly no resolution of anything that has counted up to the
point of dissolution as important or meaningful. Death can be as
random as it is brutal. It is therefore impossible to generalise
about loss in a way that will do justice to the topic, given the
particularity of each human experience of deprivation. But
while acknowledging the limitations of what can be said, and the
dangers of appropriating uniquely particular experiences in
the service of universal truths, I would like to try to convey in
this chapter some sense of what loss might amount to in the
wider context of human existence.

   Finitude is, as we have seen, embedded in the nature of the
universe of which all human beings are a part. 'The woods decay,
the woods decay and fall. The vapours weep their burthen to the
ground. Man comes and tills the fields and lies beneath. And
after many a summer dies the swan.' Exactly so. But it is the very
fact of mortality that should enable us to value what we have, in
the way of truth and beauty, to the greatest degree of intensity.
What is it that gives our lives real definition, that animates us,
that gives us colour and makes us properly rounded as people,
conferring integrity and dignity on our activities within these

limited lifespans? Such an attribute or quality is not to be found in the individualistic process of consumption, of the purchase of more and more sophisticated mobile phones, cars, clothes and comparable commodities. This process requires ever more in the way of raw materials to feed its appetite, and is inequitable in the way that it exploits others for the fuel that it needs, particularly those in the developing world, but also poorer communites closer to home. It is also in the end insatiable, since our Western lifestyles are built on a firmly established foundation of acquisitiveness. Consumption and exploitation go hand in hand here, whether it be exploitation of others poorer than ourselves for the goods that we think we require in order to maintain ecologically unsustainable communities; or rapacious exploitation of the limited resources of the earth itself – which now threatens to exact terrible revenge through climate change. It is, or should be, in our relationships with our fellows that we see reflected the nature of who we are – of our best selves. And if we value our companions – our lovers, our friends, our colleagues – as reflections of us, then by extension we will come to know our world as it really is: as a fragile and delicate environment that is dependent on us for its continuing good health, just as we are dependent on it for ours. Custodianship involves responsibility, and freedom leads to hard choices. But more than that, ours is an environment that is sanctified and hallowed, which because of its limited lifespan (every planet is doomed to extinction, even as the star that gave it life is marked for terminal combustion) deserves to be cherished simply by virtue of the fact that it will not endure. There is no such thing as forever. The ennui that follows the end of summer is but harbinger of the chill winds of autumn, which themselves announce the frosts of winter; and the varieties of beauty that we see in the seasonal cycle are contingent upon the necessary fact that nothings lasts.

But why not more life? Why should we not want more of the very thing that is so precious, and that in the end will be taken away from us, perhaps in circumstances which are cruel or humiliating, or sudden and unheralded? Why the tragic loss of life, of wasted talent, of youth or childhood cut down before it has reached its prime? In John Bowker's view, one might as well ask why the universe is happening, since life may only continue in the ways that it does if existing creatures make way for fresh manifestations of life, a process that requires the redistribution of molecular energy in death. Such questions have much engaged contemporary novelists, as well as theologians and philosophers. For instance, in his novel *The Affirmation* the writer Christopher Priest constructs an alternative world where a process called athanasia has been developed which perpetuates indefinitely the life of the human body.[1] Winners of a national lottery, called Lotterie-Collago, are entitled in Priest's novel to undergo a therapeutic process whereby the cells of the body are cleansed and renewed, resulting in perpetual agelessness – or eternal life. However, the inevitable consequence of the treatment is permanent memory loss. Recipients of the athanasia treatment are therefore in a very real sense 'born again', since their identities have to be reconstructed from records and documentation about their lives and selves that they provide before going under the anaesthetic. The narrator of the story, Peter Sinclair, decides in the end to countenance injection of the chemicals that will endow him with perennial youth and good health, but he does so with great misgiving. His reluctance is attibutable especially to the relinquishment of the therapy by a former prize-winner – an internationally famous novelist called Deloinne – by whom he has been much influenced. Sinclair's subsequent confusion, disorientation, and eventual mental and emotional breakdown, which follow on from the gradual disintegration of his whole personality, are indicative that he, like Deloinne, would have been wise to have turned athanasia down. Possibly thinking of the creative energy which animates his own startlingly original and stretching fiction, Priest writes of the Deloinne case as follows:

> As a result of his nomination, Deloinne later wrote an impassioned book called *Renunciation*. In this he argued that to accept athanasia was to deny death, and as life and death were inextricably linked it was a denial of life too. All his novels, he said, had been written in the knowledge of his inevitable death, and none could or would have been written without it. He expressed his life through literature, but this was in essence no different from the way other people expressed their own

lives. To aspire to live forever would be to acquire living at the expense of life . . . Deloinne died of cancer two years after *Renunciation* was published. It was now recognized as his greatest work, his highest literary achievement.[2]

We begin to have a sense of why loss is important in ways other than just functional ones, or so that life can simply perpetuate itself in different forms. To live for ever, to evade the process of ageing and maturing – and of learning from the wisdom that is the concomitant of this maturation – would be to cut out of life the experience of transience that gives meaning to the glory and vibrancy of living itself. Ursula Le Guin explores this issue throughout her brilliant novel *The Farthest Shore*, which I have touched on in *Why Bother with Theology?*, but which is powerful and important enough to deserve further mention. Her book is informed throughout by a sensitive and discreetly intelligent Taoist sensibility that weighs up the proper cost of the responsibilities that we owe to our companions upon life's road.[3] In Le Guin's story, the two main characters, Ged and Arren (who, as magician and king-in-waiting, in some respects approximate to Merlin and Arthur), come to appreciate more keenly than ever before how valuable and precious the mortal world is, and do so at the very gates of the kingdom of death. It is here that they must confront the enemy who has opened up a rift between the worlds of the dead and the living, thereby – in Christopher Priest's words – perpetuating 'living at the expense of life'. It is when confronted by the stark reality of what is likely to be his last task, quite possibly ending in his own death (and which does in fact cost him the loss of his art, the magic which up to this point has been the mainstay of his public office as Archmage – or Chief Wizard – of Roke, as well as the chief constituent of his whole identity) that Ged sees the world in its true guise. For it is within the silence of Selidor, the last island in the west – where 'the grass is dry and short, blowing forever and forever in the wind' – with its low hills, seemingly endless salt marshes and vast, uninhabited spaces, that he is able to hold all of creation in a gaze that expresses 'a great, wordless, grieving love'.[4] And it is by appreciating this vision of profound attachment to a world that must perish that enables Arren, Ged's companion, to see

Ged 'for the first time whole, as he was'.[5] Having perceived at first only an empty and barren island, 'as dead as the land of death itself', Arren is later able to view the world differently, as he comes to recognise a 'living splendour that was revealed around them in the silent, desolate land, as if by a power of enchantment surpassing any other'.[6] Such a transformative experience of the integral value of life and death to the landscape of the imagination – and by extension to all that is best about human artistic endeavour – comes to powerful fruition in the subsequent condemnation by Ged of his enemy, the renegade wizard Cob, a condemnation that contains the essence of Le Guin's own credo. 'Do you not understand?' asks Ged of Cob, genuinely enraged that the egotism of this one man, in seeking endless life for himself, should have brought the whole world to the edge of disaster:

> Did you never understand, you who called up so many shadows from the dead, who summoned all the hosts of the perished, even my lord Erreth-Akbe, wisest of us all? Did you not understand that he, even he, is but a shadow and a name? His death did not diminish life. Nor did it diminish him. He is there – *there*, not here! Here is nothing, dust and shadows. There, he is the earth and sunlight, the leaves of trees, the eagle's flight. He is alive. And all who ever die, live; they are reborn, and have no end, nor will there ever be an end. All, save you. For you would not have death. You lost death, you lost life, in order to save yourself.[7]

There is no doubt that in Le Guin's reckoning the concept of perpetual life constitutes an evasion of responsibility, or of the completeness of being – a selfish and immature gratification of the ego at the expense of a properly communal sense of being part of something wider and more meaningful. As she writes at one point in another of her novels, 'If you evade suffering you also evade the chance of joy. Pleasure you may get, or pleasures, but you will not be fulfilled. You will not know what it is to come home.'[8] If loss, then, is in a very real sense a precondition of a properly *fulfilled* life – and not only one of 'life yielding to life and for life', as John Bowker describes it – we begin to have a

sense of the appropriate context for our individual losses.
Certainly our world requires loss, the loss of its plants as well as
its people, in order to redistribute the energy that it needs to
continue being an inhabitable world at all. Though this is not in
any way to condone the eradication of different species, whether
of plant or animal (which is quite a different matter, and a
terrible consequence of human self-centredness), individual loss,
as well as the loss of individuals, is very much loss for the greater
good of us all. And such loss, as we see in the stories of writers
like Priest and Le Guin, may be positive, enriching experiences.
But this can never make such loss more tolerable to bear or to
understand for those who feel its effects. As Bowker so rightly
says, '*Of course* that does not make such dying easy, either to
experience or to watch. It remains true that the occasions of
death are all too often the opportunities of immense evil, and
that religious and secular vigilance is deeply necessary if death
is not to become an instrument of those who are living beyond
morality.'[9] However, despite this necessary and important pro-
viso, there is a sense that an appropriately holistic view of
loss, where we figure as individual actors in a bigger play, on a
wider stage, can take us into a sphere where loss can at least be
properly contextualised.

There is an important sense, then, in which loss may be understood as gain. Recently Peter Jackson has brought this out well in
a remarkably extended scene (almost meditative in its length and
intensity) in his Oscar-winning film adaptation of *The Return of
the King*, the final volume in Tolkien's epic. On their arrival at the
Grey Havens, Sam, Pippin and Merry express astonishment and
dismay that Frodo, as well as Bilbo, Gandalf and the elves, will
be making the last trip across the sea into the furthest West: a
journey from which there is no return, and in which they cannot
participate. This, then, is the final parting of the fellowship.
When questioned by Sam, who had thought that Frodo would be
able to enjoy the Shire for many years, after all his struggles and
efforts to consign Sauron's Ring to destruction, Frodo replies that
he too had thought so once. But it is not to be: he has been too
deeply hurt. He had tried to save the Shire, and it has been
saved, but not for him. In his book Tolkien expands on this: it
must often be like that when things are in danger. Someone must

give them up, lose them, so that others may keep them.[10] The free peoples of the West can only remain free if sacrifices are made, and we see this point made over and over again, both in Tolkien's novel and in Jackson's wonderfully evocative adaptation of it: in the death of Boromir, protecting Pippin and Merry from Saruman's marauding Uruk-hai; in the desperate courage of Eowyn, shielding the dying body of Theoden, King of Rohan, from the menacing Lord of the Nazgul; in Gandalf's last stand against the Balrog to make good his friends' escape from the mines of Moria; and in Sam's steadfast loyalty to Frodo, in the face of almost certain death, across the ashen plain of Gorgoroth on the road to Mount Doom. Loss is gain, even as gain can be loss. People give their lives up so that others may live. But those of the living who are left behind, like Sam at the Havens, know that something has been lost that can never come again, like the fading light of Lorien after the passing of the Elves to Westernesse, or the living, present friendship of Frodo himself, who has taken the same searoad in the last ship.[11]

By extension, and keeping Tolkien's meditations on loss in mind, one cannot look out from the Malverns towards the orchards of Herefordshire and appreciate a perfect summer evening without also recognising the probability that the forecasters are right and tomorrow it will rain. The consummate moment is only truly perceptible against a backdrop of weather-change. This is something that I came to understand more personally after I lost my job – and as at first it seemed, most alarmingly and distressingly, my career also – several summers ago, when I had plenty of scope to do a good deal of uninterrupted walking in the Malvern Hills while also considering my future. Having worked in publishing for fifteen years, with the remit of commissioning editor for religious studies, I had held several posts already, notably at two large and fairly prestigious secular organisations over a combined total of eleven years. My reputation as an editor was therefore by then quite well established. It would have been easy, and in one sense was tempting, to remain with either one of these organisations at different times. My position within each institution was secure, and they both offered healthy prospects and opportunities over the longer term. However, despite the presence there of the security and support networks that can often be relied upon within large businesses, I knew that to have signed up indefinitely to the corporate philosophies which both organisations expected of their commissioning editors would have led in the end to creative restrictedness of a kind which I did not wish to accept. For all their strengths and attractions (and there are a good many of them), there existed powerful assumptions within those publishers about what was and was not normative: assumptions which individuals less accepting of the hierarchism innate within many large firms were always going to find difficult. The consequence was that on two separate occasions I made the decision to break with the security offered by these secular organisations, and work for smaller and charitable religious outfits which seemingly offered a greater degree of creative freedom than their secular counterparts. The subsequent failure of my moves, with their resulting periods of unemployment, suggest limitations on both sides. For my part, it seems that I am by nature and temperament unsuited to work for Christian companies, whose paternalistic culture and arcane procedures I must admit that I do not have the patience to tolerate. For their part, it appears that the companies themselves have great difficulty in coming to terms with and taking on trust the talents and abilities of someone who has established a reputation outside the world of the Church, which almost by definition is beyond their ken.[12]

Would I turn the clock back, and take a different set of decisions, knowing the outcome of the last few years as I do? There is no doubt that the experience of operating according to the precepts of a particular kind of ecclesiastical mindset – whose rationale seems to be solely that it should exist, rather than that it should embrace reform to be better than it is – was intensely frustrating and disagreeable. But the truth is that although the experience of a year's unemployment and insecurity, as well as the feelings of violation that went with them, were just about as bad as I think such feelings can be, I would not travel in time and change things for the better, or supposedly for the better, even if I could do so. I have learned much from those experiences, especially about how power is exercised by those who have the establishment on their side. I have toughened up. I have taken chances which have led to new possibilities and intriguing new vistas. If I had stayed behind at the solid and dependable jobs which now lie irretrievably behind me – and before I took the risks which appeared to fail so conclusively – I am convinced that I would have developed less interestingly, both in my profession and as an individual prepared to embrace risk and change in order to push at the boundaries of what is and is not possible to achieve in life. Change can be profoundly unsettling and disturbing. When risks backfire it can seem as if there is nothing dependable or to be relied on. But the consequence of settling for what one already has – however limited it may seem – can be inertia, a progressive absence of challenge, and a preparedness to accept institutional norms without question, when it is precisely such norms which require critique if organisations are to grow fruitfully and with integrity in the future.

Risk, then, can be creative, constructive and character-building even when it involves loss. My loss felt bad enough, even though it involved something so relatively absorbable as a big blip in my career, which up until the point that turbulence hit had always seemed to be either climbing upwards or switched onto cruise control. But is loss able to lead also to further insights, to the sense that one may be in touch with something greater and more significant than simply a fuller sense of self? Can the transcendent be discerned here? Certainly the agonising accounts of loss that one encounters in secular writing often have a good deal more honesty and power about them than do pious religious accounts in the way that they (sometimes angrily) articulate the glory of lives that are inseparably bound up with their perishability. For instance, in November 2002 the *Guardian* published an extraordinary account by the former Communist writer (and editor of the now-defunct left-wing periodical *Marxism Today*), Martin Jacques, of his chance encounter on holiday and subsequent love affair with a woman called Hari, for whom he left his then partner of eighteen years, eventually married, and by whom he had a child called Ravi.[13] As Jacques says, although when he first met her ('the most beautiful, the most exciting, the most compelling moment of my life') he felt that he had 'known her for years, not a day', and that in conversing with Hari he had 'finally met (his) soul mate', there was little about the two of them that seemed outwardly complementary:

> On the face of it . . . we had absolutely nothing in common:
> she was dark brown, I was white, she was from the equator, I
> came from cold northern climes, she was from a developing
> country, I was from the west, she was a Hindu, I was an
> atheist, she was Indian, I was Caucasian, she was a lawyer, I
> was a writer, she was 26 and I was 47.[14]

And yet, despite the string of improbabilities, this chance
meeting, and a brief conversation with a stranger on a jungle trek
in Tioman – a small tropical island off the east coast of Malaysia
– unexpectedly metamophosed for Jacques into the defining
experience of his whole life:

> Hari turned me inside out. Work had always been the most
> important thing in my life, but no more. The meaning of my
> life was no longer *Marxism Today* (or whatever came after), but
> Hari. I loved her with an extraordinary passion and
> tenderness. I had never even vaguely loved like this before. At
> 47, I was reformed as a person. To share my life with someone
> of a different colour and from a different world obliged me to
> question all my old assumptions. Nothing was the same
> again.[15]

The risks that Jacques was prepared to take in response to
the love of his life were to play themselves out in still further
unanticipated ways, and were to propel him along unexplored
highways at exhilarating speed before finally crashing to a heart-
rending and world-destroying stop. At first, everything in
Martin's and Hari's new life together appeared to be going well.
Hari moved to England and adapted successfully to her environment, first completing a master's degree in law at King's
College London, and then landing a prestigious job in a respect-
ed firm of City lawyers. Their efforts to have a child were
rewarded almost immediately, prompting Jacques to remark –
for a Marxist, somewhat incongruously – that 'it always felt as
though our relationship was blessed, that God was looking after
our every move.' The couple began to sense that a cultural shift
might be appropriate, since Martin, increasingly bored by British
politics, wanted to write a book on Asian modernity, while it was

felt that Hari's best chance of becoming a partner lay in one of her firm's East Asian offices. Although, when moving to Hong Kong, Hari experienced the crude racism of the indigenous Chinese towards somebody who they regarded as being ethnically inferior ('People ignore me in shops. They are rude to me in restaurants. They mutter black bean shit in Cantonese when they walk past me in the street.'), the happiness that she and Jacques had together in the city was nevertheless 'wonderful':

> We were sharing Asia together, our journey through life acquiring a quite new dimension. We began to realise that our future lay in both East Asia and England. Amazingly, after more than six years together, the passion, the excitement that we had felt for each other that morning on Tioman had never worn off, never dimmed. I felt the same feelings for Hari during our time in Hong Kong as at the very beginning. Except that we had now accumulated many shared experiences and a new understanding of each other: getting to know Hari was like living in a big house, and as I turned on the light in each room, new and wonderful treasures were revealed. On the face of it we may not have had anything in common, but in reality we had everything: openness, risk-taking, radicalism, energy, a love of life and people, humour, warmth, curiosity, the world.[16]

Then, during Christmas 1999, six years after their meeting, by which time their son Ravi had been born, Hari's and Martin's shared life was shattered. Hari had an epileptic fit. Taken to hospital by ambulance, it was immediately evident that she was seriously ill. The apparent indifference to her of the hospital staff ('I am Indian, and everyone else here is Chinese', Jacques records Hari as observing) was followed the next morning by Hari's death after another seizure ('the very idea was so incomprehensible, so ridiculous, so absurd. How could it be? Hari was the definition of life') in disturbing and controversial circumstances, which at a subsequent London inquest resulted in an open verdict. At the close of his article, Jacques records sombrely that, her case having already featured much in the East Asian media and beyond, Hari's death 'will shortly be the subject of litigation in

Hong Kong'. The sense of anger and loss in Jacques' intensely moving article is palpable, not just towards the people to whom Hari was entrusted for care, and who apparently let her down, but also towards the sheer, raw, inconceivable fact of his loss of her. His life was utterly transformed by his meeting with her. Their relationship turned his life upside down. And finally the transformation that this effected ended in cataclysm. As Jacques says:

> My life started on August 21, 1993, when I discovered the most beautiful thing in the world, to love somone without limit and be loved without limit. It ended on January 2, 2000, when the person whom I loved beyond all imagination died. I was born on this earth to meet Hari. She was the meaning of my life. There is no way back after such a catastrophe. There is Ravi, my treasure, my dearest friend and companion, the greatest gift that Hari could have left me, the only reason I am still alive. He will never know his mother, but I pray he will have memories of her. She was the most remarkable human being I have ever known.[17]

The article ends with lines from Bertolt Brecht ('In the dark times will there also be singing? Yes, there will also be singing about the dark times'), which suggests – alongside the rather surprising (for *Marxism Today*'s founding editor) and seemingly mystical claim that he was born on this earth to meet Hari – that, in spite of the wrenching agony and pain of his loss, the life that Martin had with Hari is still to be celebrated and remembered joyfully. One clear implication of the piece seems to be that even though he has had to shoulder the burden of terrible, almost unbearable grief ('For the last three years, I have just about managed to stay on the right side of life, devastated by her loss, horrified by its manner, and haunted by a desperate loneliness'), Jacques wouldn't go back to a time before his meeting with Hari, since it is she who has given purpose and definition to his life, both in the living form of their son Ravi, and in the form of the memories that he, and hopefully his son too, will have of their remarkable life together. Without wishing to appropriate for questionable ends the dignified, passionate – though admirably unsentimental – account Jacques gives of his loss, an account which appears rooted in a thoroughly secular world view, it may not be inapposite to suggest (leaving aside the mention he makes of destiny and God) that there is nonetheless a notably spiritual quality in his memoir of Hari which indicates a transcendent sensibility. He points, in the historical actuality of their meeting and relationship, to a mystery that lies above and beyond its mere factual occurrence. And in his powerful and resonant testament, Hari lives on in the imaginations of those who can feel inspired by the capacity of human beings to love one another, and can detect in such a love the movings of a mysterious presence which quickens and confers meaning on all our lives, however touched by grief or disaster they may be.

Yet it remains the case that Martin Jacques has to go on living with his loss, just as all of us touched by loss or bereavement must do when that which we love is removed from us. And this can be terribly hard, as some of the world's greatest literature eloquently and sorrowfully testifies, from the furious and despairing expostulations of Job to the mournful and wistfully nostalgic yearnings of Keats in his odes, with a whole gamut of emotional and psychological outpouring in between. Often nothing can seem to compensate for loss, if the loss is large enough. 'I am hemmed in by darkness, and thick darkness covers my face,' lamented Job.[18] Similarly, for the author of Psalm 42, 'My soul is heavy with anguish . . . I am lost in a sea of wretchedness; I drown in the waters of despair.'[19] However, for all their vicissitudes, Job and the psalmists remain focused on that transcendent and animating power of their lives which is God. Job famously continued to cry to God in the midst of all his afflictions ('Oh that I knew where I might find him, that I might come even to his seat!'),[20] while the author of Psalm 13 asks to be taught patience and fortitude even in the grip of anguish: 'I will sing to the Lord at all times,' he maintains, 'even from the depths of pain.'[21] Nicholas Wolterstorff stands in the admirable tradition of Job and the psalmists when he writes movingly and powerfully – often furiously – about the death of his son Eric in a mountaineering accident in the Swiss Alps. Despite being a devout Christian, Wolterstorff never takes the easy option. He never gives God an easy ride. He offers no explanation for why

Eric – who was only 25 – has been taken from him so unexpectedly and heart-wrenchingly. All he can do is articulate his sense
of pulverising loss, which is also a testimonial to how glorious,
enriching and significant a presence his son has been in his life
up to the point of death. Memories are important in bearing adequate testimony to the uniqueness and irreplaceable precious-
ness of Eric. But they can only go so far. As Wolterstorff says, for
him 'something is over':

> Especially in places where he and I were together this sense of
> something being over washes over me. It happens not so much
> at home, but other places. A moment in our lives together of
> special warmth and intimacy and vividness, a moment when I
> specially prized him, a moment of hope and expectancy and
> openness to the future: I remember the moment. But instead of
> lines of memory leading up to his life in the present, they all
> enter a place of cold inky blackness and never come out. The
> book slams shut. The story stops, it doesn't finish. The future
> closes, the hopes get crushed. And now instead of those shiny
> moments doing things we can share together in delighted
> memory, I, the survivor, have to bear them alone.
>   So it is with memories of him. They all lead into that
> blackness. It's all over, over, over. All I can do is *remember* him,
> I can't experience him. The person to whom those memories
> are attached is no longer here with me, standing up. He's only
> in my memory now, not in my life. Nothing new can happen
> between us. Everything is sealed tight, shut in the past. I'm
> still here. I have to go on. I have to start over. But this new
> start is so different from the first. Then I wasn't carrying this
> load, this thing that's over.
>   Sometimes I think that happiness is over for me. I look at
> photos of the past and immediately comes the thought: that's
> when we were still happy. But I can still laugh, so I guess that
> isn't quite it. Perhaps what's over is happiness as the
> fundamental tone of my existence. Now sorrow is that.
> Sorrow is no longer the islands but the sea.[22]

The best accounts of loss never downplay it. Loss through
death, in particular, can be crushing. John Bowker rightly says,

even while he acknowledges its necessity, that 'Death kills. And grief knows it.'[23] Like Bowker, Nick Wolterstorff, whom I was fortunate enough to get to know quite well in the course of publishing his books, is a person of singular sensitivity and humanity, and I respect him profoundly not so much for his 'serious' philosophical writings (which are nevertheless excellent) as for his almost brutally honest capacity to articulate his innermost heart in a popular form that has resonance for those of us who recognise that Christianity – though it may often think that it has – does not have all, or even any of, the answers. Why is it that our loved ones suffer and die? In emulation of the sufferings of Christ, by whom they will be redeemed? Is that good enough? Can one ever be complacent about a single death, in the light of doctrinal notions of atonement or redemption? No – one cannot. As Wolterstorff laments, 'I am at an impasse; and you, O God, have brought me here':

> Noon has darkened. As fast as she could say, 'He's dead', the light dimmed. And where are you in this darkness? I learned to spy on you in the light. Here in this darkness I cannot find you. If I had never looked for you, or looked but never found, I would not feel this pain of your absence. Or is it not your absence in which I dwell but your elusive and troubling presence?[24]

In the middle of his despair Wolterstorff is still able to detect God's presence. That, perhaps, like Job's, is the measure of his stature – in that, despite all the indications to the contrary, he is able to sense that God is with him. In my last book I explored what it might mean to feel the presence of God when one is thoroughly miserable and wretched, particularly in the thought and film-making of the Russian film director Andrei Tarkovsky.[25] I suggested there that there is a 'meaning' and value in reaching rock bottom, and in coming right to the limits of endurance, that is echoed here by Wolterstorff, and earlier too by Ursula Le Guin when she claims, in a way that is paradoxical and difficult, that 'the reality of pain is not pain'.[26] But the paradox of loss – and the interdependent duality of loss/gain – is hard to grasp, when our sense of personal loss so outweighs any more generalised

understanding we might have that loss is the inevitable concomitant of living. Somehow, in life, we need to find ways of
accommodating loss. A more respectful and pronounced appreciation of what we have, of the glory of the natural world and of
its manifestations, might be one way. In just this manner the poet
Alexander Blok urges us, in the face of irrevocable dissolution, to
'learn to taste another joy':

> Look into the Arctic Circle with attentive eye;
> Take your small boat, sail to the distant pole
> Between ice walls, and quietly forget
> What used to be a land of many passions,
> And how they loved there, came to grief, and fought.
>
> And teach your weary soul how to understand
> The trembling of the slowly freezing air
> So that out here it won't need anything
> When beams of light dart back from over there![27]

But if Blok's exhortation to retreat to an icy wilderness (actual
or metaphorical), devoid of the mess of living, is in many ways
attractive, it suffers from the limitations of most such retreats: it
offers a solution to dealing with loss that is based on disengage-
ment from – rather than creative and constructive dialogue with
– the world and its problems. There is an important role for
solitary contemplation in life, not least because we need to
develop an appropriate reverence for our individual connectedness with the wider environment that we inhabit, and how that
connectedness impacts on our sense of personal responsibility
towards it. But in the end, our world stands or falls on the relationships which we develop with each other, and on how we put
those relationships into practice. Personal concerns are merely
the precursor to political interests, since our behaviour as individuals has a direct impact on the well-being and security of our
neighbours (though this is a connection which for many people
in the UK appears to be a difficult one to make, if current voter
apathy is anything to go by.) Another way to accommodate loss
might consist in the *celebration* of the lives of those we love,
which in their various ways, even while they rail against the

injustice, human or divine, which led to those losses, Martin Jacques and Nick Wolterstorff try to do in respect of Hari and Eric. And in *remembering* those lives we try to celebrate them appropriately, even while recognising – as Wolterstorff does – that memory can only take us so far, and that we cannot recover the uniquely animate personhood of those we have lost.

We carry the world through our remembrance of it: in testimonies, histories, oral accounts and other writings and recordings of those we have loved and those we have lost. We tell stories about what was most beautiful, valuable and rememberable about what we have been parted from, just as we try to learn lessons (though we rarely do) from the past mistakes and errors of those who have gone before us. In our memories and our recollections based on them we recognise ourselves. And as so often, it is in contemporary *secular* descriptions of remembrance that we come to appreciate the transcendent nature of the human spirit – over adversity, loss and struggle. In this regard, the work of the playwright Stephen Poliakoff offers an especially powerful testimonial to the redemptive power of recollection. His television dramas *The Lost Prince, Shooting the Past* and – most particularly – *Perfect Strangers* all touch on the theme of memory, and in their various ways suggest that it is through memory that people finally come to understand who they are. *Perfect Strangers* makes an impressive case for being Poliakoff's finest work, not least because of the strong cast and fine acting which underpin its central themes.[28]

The primary setting of the drama is an elegant central London hotel, where a party is being hosted by Ernest Symon, patriarch of the Symon clan, a Jewish 'dynasty' ('a sort of mini-Rothschilds', as one character later describes them) whose wealth and power is unevenly distributed. The party is being held to mark the disposal of the two remaining family properties in the capital, and offer family members the opportunity to find, before these are thrown away, mementoes or artefacts which feature or might interest them. Thus the stage is set for the fundamental conceit of the drama, which is the unlocking of memories which lead to revelations and fresh insights about themselves on the part of the various characters involved.

In a clever matrix of interlocking stories, Poliakoff introduces us to Raymond Symon, his wife Esther, and his son Daniel (the self-designated 'Hillingdon contingent'), to Daniel's glamorous and slightly older cousins Rebecca and Charles, to Stephen, the family's 'archivist' (who keeps records and photographs of the family history), and to Alice, glamorous aunt to Charles and Rebecca and, as we later discover, their former guardian and protector. A dinner party for the guests leads to a sort of informal karaoke session, where family members are invited up to the rostrum to recount stories and anecdotes about their lives. Raymond does so, but with disastrous consequences. Feeling acutely sensitive about the dubious reputation he thinks he has acquired for losing his father's fortune in a business misadventure, and assuming that he is viewed by his high society relatives as a rather dull and unsuccessful suburban 'black sheep', he gets drunk and delivers a rambling and self-justificatory (though ultimately poignant) monologue which culminates in his suffering a stroke. To his chagrin he is housed in Ernest's flat (one of the two family properties to be sold) to recuperate. Meanwhile, his son Daniel falls in with Charles and Rebecca, and discovers that, despite their former closeness to Alice, the two of them have not communicated with her for many years. Rebecca's request that he act as a go-between for herself and Alice brings to light Rebecca's resentment that her brother Richard – who we learn died in a train accident, following an illness several years before – has been left off the party's guest list, an omission which Rebecca (mistakenly, as it turns out) attributes to a deliberate gesture of disavowal on Alice's part.

Daniel feels that he can make a difference in this complex emotional interplay by effecting reconciliation between Alice and his cousins. He tricks Rebecca – with whom, despite her misgivings, he has begun an affair, and who sees a strong resemblance between him and her dead brother Richard – into attending a subsequent garden party for Ernest's niece Martina. In the meantime, it has become clear that Richard's omission from the guest-list was a genuine mistake; that Rebecca, Charles and Alice all feel terrible guilt for cutting Richard out of their lives as a result of his illness (a sort of manic, obsessive-compulsive disorder), which accounts for Rebecca's resentful rejection of Alice; and that it is precisely because of their former closeness – their

parents had no interest in Charles, Richard or Rebecca, which
is why Alice took them under her wing – that any ongoing intimacy between them has now, at least for Rebecca and Charles,
become intolerable.

Upon discovering Alice in the rotunda of the house's extensive
gardens, during the preliminary stages of Martina's party,
Rebecca rejects both Alice and Daniel in tearful fury, stating cat-
egorically that she wishes never to have contact with Alice again.
But at the later marquee dinner, Alice (played with great poise
and dignity by Lindsay Duncan), takes the opportunity to pay
tribute in her welcome speech to 'my friend Richard, who I loved
as a child . . . *as my own child* . . . and who is not with us any
more'.[29] This unexpected and moving tribute takes Rebecca by
surprise, and suggests that, despite what has seemed to be an
impossible breach in her and Alice's relationship, reconciliation
and renewed friendship might be achieved after all. Richard is
publicly remembered and value is attributed to him and to his
life, and in that process he is reintegrated into the heart of a community that had apparently rejected him.[30] Daniel's intervention
has seemingly paid dividends after all, even though any continuation of his own relationship with Rebecca remains unresolved.
A true account of life means that even in stories of redemption
the remaining loose ends don't always get tied up.

Such a summary hardly does justice to the richness and muti-
faceted texture of Poliakoff's drama, because accompanying the
central narrative about Alice, Rebecca and Daniel are a series of
surrounding vignettes which reinforce the idea that memory is
fundamental to who and what we are. Stephen tells Daniel that
his obsession with family trees may be traced back to the fact
that his mother was compelled to memorise an invented list of
names and places in order to conceal her Jewish identity from the
Nazis in wartime Germany. Esther is inspired by Stephen's
archives to look into her own provenance and heritage, and discovers that her predilection for garden pinnacles and towers
may be traced back to an ancestor, William Beckford, who had an
obsession for building parkland follies. Raymond (marvellously
played by Michael Gambon) is intrigued by the photographs
that Stephen produces of Raymond's father, Lionel, which show
the latter gaily dancing in a curious huntsman's or pixie's outfit,

and whose clothes and behaviour seem altogether out of character, at least as Raymond remembers him. At first believing that
his father was dancing for him, Raymond comes to understand
that in fact he was performing for his, Lionel's, sister-in-law
Henrietta, who was hidden in the trees, invisible in the photos
(since it was she who took them), and with whom he was having
a passionate affair. This revelation intersects with Daniel himself
being shown a photograph by Stephen which depicts him,
Daniel, as a child in the fancy costume of a little prince. At first
he cannot recall on what occasion the fancy dress party might
have taken place, but his subsequent discovery of one of the
decorated shoes that he is wearing in the photo, and then his
encounter with the mural which the photo replicates, lead him to
understand that it was his grandfather, and Raymond's father,
who took him to the party as a 'love token' to Lionel's erstwhile
love, Henrietta, who was by then in her seventies. For it was in
the building where the revelatory mural is housed, close to the
location for Martina's engagement party, as well as the setting
for the drama's denouement, that Lionel and Henrietta would go
to make love, in a secret tryst, all those years ago. Their love-
making was overseen by the mural of the little prince, forming
an unforgettable association in the minds of them both, and
'remembered' many years later, when their affair had ended, in
the form of Lionel's offering to his former lover of Daniel in the
little prince's clothes, which exactly imitated those of the mural.

Perhaps the most remarkable of Poliakoff's inventive and
interlocking stories concerns the three elderly Symon sisters,
Violet, Edith and Grace. The peripatetic adventures in the war of
the younger sisters Edith and Violet, when they roamed the
countryside stealing food from farms, having run away from
their parents and elder sister, leads Daniel to understand that
Richard's tragic illness was inherited, and that nothing could
have been done about it. 'There's this pattern in the family,' he
tells Alice, Rebecca and Charles with quiet authority, *a pattern
that recurs*.[31] He continues:

> if you know anything about the story of Violet and Edith, how
> they lived in the woods during the war, how they removed
> themselves from their parents and sister, how they've been in a

different world ever since really, *it's in the family* – don't you
see! . . . And it came out again in Richard. This force pulling
him away, and once it had reappeared, it was bound to happen
– him growing away from you and everybody, there was
nothing you could have done . . . nobody could have stopped
it.[32]

Guilt is a central motif in this drama, and is not confined just
to Rebecca, Alice and Charles. Raymond seems to feel guilty that
he has let his father down, and pushed the family firm to bank-
ruptcy by adopting a deliberate (and as he later sees it, irrespon-
sible) policy of hiring only workers over the age of fifty during
a recession (a policy which at different points he describes as
both a 'bold experiment' and more self-condemningly as a
'disaster', but which Alice, with compassionate insight, more
charitably characterises as a 'defiant . . . gesture against the
times'[33]). Raymond's guilt is manifested in his obvious irritation
and subsequent heavy drinking when several members of the
Symon family solicitously ask him at the reunion party whether
he and his financial affairs are quite 'all right'. But he later comes
to understand that his father, whom he had always seen as
'driven', and setting impossibly high standards, was as capable
of passionate defiance – in this case, in his affair with Henrietta
and his joyful dancing for her while dressed in the pixie costume
– as Raymond was in his business recruitment policy and general unwillingness to fall in with convention. As Raymond later
says to Daniel, 'To find he was so full of passion – it was adul-
terous, he betrayed my mother – but it makes him a lot more
easy to cope with, I can tell you! I can start judging *him* for a
change!'[34] Similarly, Alice, Rebecca and Charles all guiltily feel
that they betrayed Richard in the way they treated him just
before he died. But they come to see from the corresponding tale
of Violet and Edith, the wild children roaming the countryside
during the war, that however they had behaved towards
Richard, whether they had cut him out of their lives, or not, they
were powerless to affect the innate strain in Richard that led him
to grow away from people: a built-in tendency that led in the end
to his death. Correspondingly, Daniel (who starts to feel uneasy
about his compromised relationships with both Rebecca and

Alice) discovers that just as he was a 'love-token' and go-
between for Lionel and Henrietta as a child, so as an adult he has
been a go-between for Alice and Rebecca, as well as a 'love-
token' for the latter, who appears to recognise in him similar
qualities to those of her dead brother, Richard. The past is being
recapitulated in the present, and in their different ways the pro-
tagonists all come to understand that they cannot define themselves apart from who and where they have come from: and also
that the guilt that they feel may in some way be neutralised and
made good by such definition. For Poliakoff, redemption is
always a real possibility, and can affect surprising and long-last-
ing transformation, not just in the lives of individuals, but also of
whole families and communities.

At the beginning of the drama these characters all feel that
they have lost some part of themselves, whether it be a relationship that defined them, or a sense of comprehension of what
really motivates them, or an intriguing recollection of themselves
that they cannot place. By the end of the story, they have a gathering sense that they are not strangers to themselves, or to each
other, after all, since it is through a proper comprehension of
their memories of and relationships with their relatives that they
arrive at true (or perfect) self-insight. The title of the piece, *Perfect
Strangers*, is therefore full of affectionate irony, and it is fitting
that the drama concludes with Alice's toast to 'all of us' and a
photocall for the whole family, who are captured at last, not in
the separate photos by which, individually, they have been tan-
talised throughout, but in a large ensemble in which they all are
present and properly reunited.

Perfect Strangers shows, perhaps more effectively than any
other contemporary piece of writing that I know, that memories,
although they can at first be deceptive, play an essential part in
reclaiming who we are, and where we have come from.
Appropriately contextualised and understood, they put a fresh
complexion on where we are now. It is in the recollection of our
pasts, and the pasts of others, through storytelling and remembrance, that we hold on to what we have lost, and can make
sense of that loss in the present, either through public restitution
(in the case of Alice's tribute to Richard) or in private reflection,
as in Stephen's realisation that his obsession with the Symon

family archives is based not on trivial interest, but is directly inspired by a case of life and death: that of his mother's brave and necessary deception to avoid deportation to Auschwitz. In holding on to who we are, and from where we have come, we have a vision of a world we have lost that is nevertheless touchable and tangible, to the extent that it can still impact on our lives in the here and now. And in understanding that impact, we come into contact – as in Poliakoff's drama – with qualities like love, loyalty and repentance which are at least as much religious as they are secular themes. At one point or another, all the characters in *Perfect Strangers* encounter a sense of themselves that transcends their individuality: they are part of something greater than merely their own preferences, prejudices and preoccupations. We come to see that the meaning of their lives is profoundly bound up with a gathering sense of connectedness to their different pasts (which is actually the same past) and to a web of linkages that bind them together, not just as a family, but to the wider struggles and encounters of all human beings. With self-knowledge comes a sense of integratedness, of being part of something bigger and more enduring than their own selves and limitations. And with that insight comes reconciliation: between people who were formerly estranged, and also of the same people to their own failings, which now, properly and holistically contextualised, become at last explicable and transformative.

Loss, then, can lead us to a discovery of who we are. The loss of that which we cherish, whether those whom we love or, more mundanely, a job which we might value, all contribute in the end to the sense of relationship that we have with things, which are also things-beyond-themselves. There is a mystery at the heart of existence which defies easy categorisation. There is a limit beyond which language cannot go. What language, and more particularly stories (like Poliakoff's), can do is show us the track that lies ahead, and point towards a horizon which conceals others who have gone before us. Storytelling gives colour to the flowers along the roadside, but it does not necessarily tell us what lies at the end of the road itself. In our memories of that which we had, we try to contextualise our losses into something which in the end becomes livable. In memory lies the connection

that establishes our humanity, that commonality that stretches
back to some atavistic proto-memory of shared endeavour in the
landscape of time and risk. And it is in this landscape that, as
Ursula Le Guin has expressed it, 'the spirit may, with luck and
courage, construct the fragile, makeshift, improbable roads and
cities of fidelity: a landscape inhabitable by human beings.'[35] In
losing what we love, we may seem to lose part of ourselves; but
in losing one aspect of that which we are, it may be possible to
gain another – so loss is gain, even as gain may be loss, as we
have seen throughout this chapter. There is no progress without
risk, no wisdom or experience without ageing and dissolution, in
the end no life without death. Loss is the inevitable concomitant
of life. But in living life at its fullest, at its most gloriously unpredictable, and perhaps sorrowful, extent – life at its most *vibrant-
ly alive* – we appreciate loss for what it is: the measure of who we
are as human beings.

In a notable novel published in 1987 called *The Levels*, Peter
Benson writes about a sixteen-year-old boy, Billy, who falls in
love, during a memorable summer in the Somerset Levels, with
Muriel, a girl his own age, who is temporarily visiting the area
from London. In his story Benson manages to convey, with
an exquisitely crafted perfection, the bittersweet experience of
making love for the first time, which all of us who recall our
own first, tentative experiences of love and loss will probably
recognise with a sense of haunting resonance:

> It is private, what we did, but I cannot let it pass without the
> memory crying back from that past, of her sweetness and the
> lust she displayed. How such sweetness could breed that
> gentle violence, when the field folded us in, and the sheep
> anxious for their lives, relaxed at our pleasure . . . I could not
> do it for long, I remembered that, but in my remembering,
> think it went on longer. I pictured each moment, and it's like I
> have them framed, so now I cannot lose the pleasure I felt. We
> didn't get dressed for a while, she lay in the crook of my arm,
> the soft hairs on her legs playing in the breeze, the whistle of a
> herding farmer and the bark of his dog, blowing to us on the
> air of our love. A swan, flying, a cow, lowing, and the tiny
> rustles of the hedge, this music, and the music of the river,

played at my first loving, and I cannot bear to think now 'I am alone' when somewhere someone carries the afterburn of my seed.[36]

At the end of Benson's novel Muriel returns to the city, leaving the boy bereft and consumed by that peculiar sense of loss and abandonment which are perhaps more germane to adolescence than any other time:

> Muriel. I lay in bed, trying to sleep but I couldn't. I watched the moon trace patterns on the ceiling, listened to the call of owls and a dog barking, miles away across the quiet and sad moor of that memory. I thought about her, lying in bed at Drove House, warm, still. Her hair on another pillow, her body in clean sheets; that memory, a grieving, mysterious thing.[37]

The intensity of Billy's first love is matched by the correspondent emptiness of his loss. And therefore his memory of Muriel will for ever be with him and part of him. To live is to love, and to love is to lose. But the paradox of such loss is that it will be with him always, since his memory of making love with Muriel for the first time will forever evoke associations that linger. Questions of loss and love are inextricably bound up, and it is therefore to love that I want to turn in the next chapter.

CHAPTER 3

Love

En la tarde, te examinaran en el amor.
'When evening comes, they will examine you in love.'
St John of the Cross

*Does he love me? Does he love anyone more than me? Does he love
me more than I love him? Perhaps all the questions we ask of love, to
measure, test, probe, and save it, have the additional effect of cutting
it short. Perhaps the reason we are unable to love is that we yearn to
be loved, that is, we demand something (love) from our partner
instead of delivering ourselves up to him demand-free and asking for
nothing but his company.*
Milan Kundera, from *The Unbearable Lightness of Being*

*Remember me when I am gone away,
Gone far away into the silent land;
When you can no more hold me by the hand.
Nor I half turn to go yet turning stay.
Remember me when no more day by day
You tell me of our future that you plann'd:
Only remember me; you understand
It will be too late to counsel then or pray.*
Christina Rossetti, from 'Remember'

*Go back, go back. Back to the hottest summer of the nineties. All day the
sun has blazed and pulsed and scorched. Outside on the capital's*

streets, on which the haze lies heavy, where tar melts in peeling strips, and food is decaying in casually discarded piles, the anthemic songs of Britpop – Blur, Oasis, the Boo Radleys – blare from the radios of innumerable taxis, cars and vans. Here, after many years' exile, is my first real experience of being, of living, in London. And here too, in a cavernous room overlooking the shaded square of the university, where my lover is writing up her doctorate, I can inhale the scents of a city that is putting its siesta to one side and gearing up for the festivities of evening. As the bedroom curtain wafts upwards in delicate airlifts, and the sunlight of late afternoon bakes the stonework of my girlfriend's first-floor balcony, the muffled laughter and laconic greetings of the students in the square below ascend through the treetops and opened french windows like communications from some other world. I can taste from further away the brackish effluence of exhaust and petrol, as vehicles race at speed towards Knightsbridge and Hyde Park, and the roar of traffic mixes with the cries and fractured talk of a stretching and awakening metropolis getting ready to face the night. It is 1995, and I am in love, as never before, with life, with London, and with her.

In the long distance of that distant room, lost over the gulf of intervening years, I remember my lover as she was: her burnished beauty that never failed to catch my breath; her chestnut eyes; her satin skin that semed to glow – I recall her radiant physicality, captured in a perfect moment when time itself rolled back and ceased. I remember the burning night-time of that bright and languorous London summer. The golden light has faded, and the walls of that room are shadowed now. In the tunnelled recess of memory, telescoping backwards towards an entrance that recedes, dim shapes loom up to provoke and tantalise, then dance away like storm flies on the wind.

Years later, I went back to walk the streets where she and I had walked. I looked up at the room where she and I had loved, filled now with other voices, other lives. That pizzeria we used to eat at and – ah, yes: still there! – the patisserie on the corner with the luxurious cakes, I recognise those. But she and I were absent from this tableau. A laugh, a word, a touch – those moments of eternity. Too soon, yet too late. What remained were echoes. I could sense, but not see. Somewhere, somehow, that time remained unsullied by the sweat of intervening years. It existed in some other sphere, made real by recollection. Everything fades, nothing is permanent. But whoever and wherever I am, you will always be part of me now. That is your immortality.

If it is in our relationships with others that we come nearest to a sense of who we really are, and are shown what our fundamental meanings of life might consist of, then it is in those relationships with the people to whom we are closest that we have the content of such meanings shown to us most intensely and affectingly. Love: what is it and where does it come from? For millennia these questions have taxed humanity. But it has been argued that the notion of love as the acme of emotional self-expression is a relatively recent phenomenon. The Greeks, for instance, had many words for love, and as Ziyad Marar observes, it is 'only in modern times that we have decided to merge these diverse strands into the quixotic ambition of "true love"'.[1] Love has many manifestations, therefore, both inward and external: love of a lover, of a spouse, of a cause, of one's country, of one's friends and supporters, for example, as well as love for one's own abilities and ambitions and advancement. Love is often difficult to separate from self-love, and that is when love is but a short step away from the desire to dominate others for the sake of oneself and one's own motivations, which leads to the opposite of love: self-orientation, hatred and lust for power. Love and hate – such a narrow distance from one to the other, yet across a chasm that so often seems immeasurable. Such is one of the central paradoxes of our lives.

Despite the admonitions of Jesus and St Paul, people now have as much trouble with love, and with loving one another, as they did in first-century Palestine. War and violence are as prevalent and bloody in the twenty-first century as they have always been, if bitter regional conflicts like those in Chechnya and the Sudan (as well as what progressively looks like a titanic and long-term stand-off between the Western democracies and radical Islam) are used as yardsticks to measure by. After the fall of the Berlin Wall and the end of the Cold War – and all the latter's attendant anxieties about nuclear devastation – there was a period during the 1990s, and up to the start of the millennium, when it looked as if America's geopolitical hegemony, under the leadership of a Democrat president with multilateralist instincts, might initiate a new era of global peace and prosperity, despite the evident inequalities of the capitalistic process. All that changed with 9/11, and the subsequent military and moral crusade of a Republican administration driven by neo-imperialist ambitions (underscored by an apocalyptic rhetoric about the USA's God-given mandate) to impose unilateral solutions on complex geopolitical problems.[2]

The climate of anger and intercultural suspicion that has since reigned will probably mean a bitter legacy for our children. Whole societies increasingly start to feel under siege, whether they be the majority populaces of the West who are psychologically as well as physically vulnerable to terrorism, or, more poignantly, the large majority of moderate Western Muslims who denounce violence, and who are victimised and abused because of the uncompromising and hateful mindset of a radical foreign minority. Failure of love, and of the mutual understanding which goes hand in hand with it, almost by definition is the greatest of human deficiencies. To love is to open up part of oneself to another or others in a way that exposes the fragility of our psychological and emotional make-up. The vulnerability which results from such exposure, and of reaching out to the other, is consequent on our having to let go of the props and supports which maintain us in our isolation, and which so often ring-fence and guard our sense of self-worth. Without love, we fear and despise what we do not understand. That is why love is so prized, precious and hard won (because relinquishment of our defences is tantamount to self-surrender), but also so dangerous (because in the process we seem to leave ourselves wide open to invasion).

When I consider my own past relationships, I know that to reach out to somebody in honesty and trust, and in a respectful spirit of wanting to push at the boundaries of reciprocity, is to offer someone some innermost part of oneself. Without that desire to trust, and thereby to reveal one's most secret life and character, no partnership is likely to endure. To love is to open and be opened up. To love is to relinquish one's often hard-won sense of self-sufficiency. To love is to lose but also to win. For it is in love that we see our world renewed, and imbued with a fresh essence, even while our old assumptions and predilections die and wither away. Yet love can fail, as it has for me more than once, and sometimes with a sense of anguished wastefulness and 'what ifs'. Love is about risk and heartbreak and potential ruin as much as about satisfaction or contentment. To walk certain London streets is still fraught, for me, with danger. I can feel myself sucked down those byways and mews which are shadowed and haunted by past ghosts. The risk of ambush is ever present. Yet would I change the past, if I could, for the sake of ridding myself of old regrets? For the sake of exorcising the sadness and loss which sometimes feel like a bitter assault? I must say no, because it was in those moments whose passing I now mourn that I felt that I knew myself most supremely and intensely. And such insight came only because I feel that I recognised, with all too human fears and misgivings, that to have is not necessarily always to hold.

In the present climate more and more people seem to grapple, in a confused and troubled state of disenfranchisement, with the challenge of finding love for themselves. This individual fragmentation in relationships is reflected in a more generalised fissure between states and cultures. The established norms of expectation and of society have broken down (though sometimes, it must be said, for the better), with the nuclear family unit no longer the benchmark that it once was. Divorce is widespread, and broken families almost the norm. Single homes are on the increase, and statistics suggest that more than 6.5 million people (or 28 per cent of households) now live on their own – three times as many as forty years ago.[3] With the implacable logic of the marketplace, choice has itself become just another commodity, and is sometimes applied as relentlessly to relationships as it is to fashion: select a new pair of shoes and a partner that you like the look of, then switch your mobile and your lover when you get tired of them and feel like a change. It is no great surprise that in a climate where love increasingly is reduced to a kind of barter, the formerly desirable goal of achieving a lasting partnership has become so difficult, and indeed is often seen to be unattainable.

Younger people especially are restless, suspicious of the value of institutions like marriage, often have no great expectations of love and of a central, defining partnership, and frequently look elsewhere altogether for locales of 'meaning'. This might be to various kinds of high-octane activity where they can express themselves most intensively as well as communally (such as adventure sports like surfing and rock climbing, or club culture and travel), but also and most obviously to the consumption of various kinds of goods. I have written of this phenomenon elsewhere and have tried to draw some conclusions about the sorts of priorities which it reveals in people's lives.[4] Certainly the rise of the alternative spiritualities that we have seen in recent years, and to which I refer in the introduction,[5] is related to this febrile consumerism. While of course it is in one sense a reaction against the marketplace (with a view to recovering some sense of authenticity that is not dependent on acquisitiveness), it is also inseparable from the market's imperatives and intrinsic rationale. The New Age is the flip side of global capitalism and, without the farrago of choice that globalisation offers to Western consumers, it would in all probability cease to exist in its present extraordinary variety of forms. A recent advertisement for a camera phone in the London lifestyle magazine *Time Out* seems to sum up the mood of the Zeitgeist. An attractive young woman with total self-absorption is shown pointing the mobile at her own face, while the strap-line reads: 'Shoot what you love.' The love that is being promoted as the most desirable acquisition for modern urbanites appears to consist of a kind of narcissistic, voyeuristic self-promotion, articulated via the purchase of a mobile upgrade.

Of course, such banality is not the whole story. Despite the inability of the churches by and large to make their central message attractive to upcoming generations,[6] we see plenty of evidence in the work of recent secular artists – novelists and film-makers particularly – of different and more inspiring expressions of love, in which glimpses of the transcendent may certainly be discerned. And what I want to explore now, continuing with the theme of the last chapter, is the complex interrelationship of love and memory that seems to highlight an especially meaningful aspect of our lives, one where we can find areas of authentic spirituality. In concentrating upon novels and film, I want to reinforce the idea that it is in *telling stories* that we try perennially to make sense of the world, and to bind ourselves to it in a way that discerns 'meaning' and purpose in what we see and hear.

How can we find meaning in love? This is a question that pre-occupies some of the best and most interesting contemporary directors and writers. For instance, in his novel *Birdsong*, Sebastian Faulks is preoccupied throughout (and not just in the passage examined in Chapter 1[7]) with the question of what con-stitutes meaning in the midst of carnage and apparent futility, where countless lives are squandered for the sake of yards of earth. Faulks concentrates on the experiences of the British officer Stephen Wraysford, whose perceptions and analysis of the war are defined throughout by his past affair with a French woman called Isabelle Fourmentier, who temporarily left her abusive husband for Stephen, only to return to her spouse when the weight of guilt and broken convention compelled her to retreat from her new life. Although he has been abandoned by Isabelle, it is to the memory of this woman that Stephen resorts in those moments of extremity and danger when he feels closest to death. In the agonising hours before the battle of the Somme, Stephen – like so many of the young soldiers for whom he is responsible – pens a few lines which indicate, to a greater degree perhaps than anything else he says or does, the driving force behind his existence:

> Dear Isabelle, I am sending this to you at the house in Amiens where it will probably be destroyed, but I am writing to you because I have no one else to write to. I am sitting beneath a tree near the village of Auchonvillers where once we came to spend a day.
>
> Like hundreds of thousands of British soldiers in these fields I am trying to contemplate my death. I write to say that you are the only person I have ever loved.
>
> This letter will probably never find you, but I wanted to tell someone what it feels like to be sitting on this grass, on this Friday in June, feeling the lice crawl against my skin, my stomach filled with hot stew and tea, perhaps the last food I will eat, and hearing the guns above me crying to heaven.
>
> Some crime against nature is about to be committed. I feel it in my veins. These men and boys are grocers and clerks,

gardeners and fathers – fathers of small children. A country cannot bear to lose them.

I am frightened of dying. I have seen what shells can do. I am scared of lying wounded all day in a shellhole. Isabelle, I am terribly frightened I shall die alone with no one to touch me. But I have to show an example.

I have to go over first in the morning. Be with me, Isabelle, be with me in spirit. Help me to lead them into what awaits us.

With my love always, Stephen.[8]

This extraordinary invocation of a past lover has about it the simple truth and authentic power of prayer, and it moves us so much because it is motivated not by any practical desire of self-exoneration, or by a hope of self-delivery, as by the earnest, heartfelt necessity to proclaim things as they are. Despite being in the midst of a war and surrounded by his fellow soldiers, Stephen feels isolated and alone. There is a likelihood of death in what is to come. He needs above all to tell her that he loves her. And in what follows, Stephen is indeed sustained by the memories that he has of Isabelle and of the life that they shared briefly before the war. Even in the midst of battle, he is capable of achieving a kind of transcendent separation from the slaughter, when the trenches roll back, and he can see a world beyond them:

Alive, he thought, dear God, I am alive. The war lifted from him. It is just a piece of field beneath a French heaven, he thought. There are trees beyond the noise, and down in the valley is the fish-filled river.[9]

At a later stage of the novel, having survived several sorties and dangers, Stephen unexpectedly encounters Isabelle through the mediation of her sister Jeanne. It emerges both that Isabelle's beauty has been marked and permanently scarred by shelling that ripped through her house in Amiens, disfiguring her face, and that she has fallen in love with an officer called Max, who arrived with the German forces which for a while occupied her city. Stephen's meeting with Isabelle is not what he expected, in that he discovers not only that she still lives (which was in some doubt), but that she is now also the lover of one of the enemy soldiers. Although there is still an erotic charge in their encounter, Stephen knows, as he makes his way back to the front, that this will be the last time they will see each other. Initially it seems that his summonings of the memory of Isabelle have been pointless, since the legacy of their love consists only of a shared recollection of a passion that is no longer possible or sustainable in the present. But despite this knowledge, Stephen realises that he can live with the loss of Isabelle in the process of his ongoing existence. He comes to understand that their love (which we are left in no doubt has been the central and compelling experience of his life) still exists, but in a place and form removed from the grime of war and destruction – and also from the inevitable small compromises that constitute any enduring human relationship:

> Jeanne wrote to say that Isabelle had left Amiens to go to Munich, where her German had returned home after being badly wounded. Max had had to pay an enormous sum to get her out through Switzerland. Isabelle had said goodbye to her and would never return to France. She was an outcast in her parents' family and in the town . . .
> Stephen laid the letter down on the rough surface of the table, in the grooves of which the rat's blood had died. Then he rested his head in his hands. He had received an answer to the simple question that had intrigued him. Isabelle no longer loved him; or if she did, she loved him in some distant way that did not affect her actions or her feelings for another man.
> When he looked into his reserves of strength he found that he could bear this thought. He told himself that the feeling they had had for each other still existed, but that it existed at a different time.
> Once when he had stood in the chilling cathedral in Amiens he had foreseen the numbers of the dead. It was not a premonition, more a recognition, he told himself, that the difference between death and life was not one of fact but merely of time. This belief had helped him bear the sound of the dying on the slopes of Thiepval. And so he was now able

to believe that his love for Isabelle, and hers for him, was safe
in its extreme ardour – not lost, but temporarily alive in a
manner as significant as any present or future state of feeling
could be in the long darkness of death.[10]

For Stephen Wraysford the love he has had for Isabelle reveals
to him something about the meaning of being alive. Some experiences are not repeatable. It is the very nature of their exclu-
sivity, of their unique and non-replicable qualities, which makes
them as profound, magnificent, and emotionally resonant as
they are. The impact of this love affair upon his life has been
incalculable, to the degree that it actually transcends time. Their
love for one another still exists, but in a transcendent dimension
that is accessible now only through reflection and remembrance.
The transcendent breaks through into Stephen's existence
through the ripples that subsequently spread outwards from this
relationship, and suffuse every facet of his current life, like the
aftershocks of an earthquake. He cannot experience this relationship in the present moment; but its presence on the plane of
memory means that it now affects everything that he is and does.
In a significant sense, then, his love for Isabelle, like hers for him,
is as current and as immanent as it has always been. And it is this
insight which teaches Stephen that – when measured against the
ultimate finitude of death – all life and love can only be assessed
by how they look from this side of a more generalised ending,
beyond whose boundaries and silent borders we cannot see. His
own experience of love and loss, which has scarred him as sear-
ingly as any bullet or shell, helps Stephen to contextualise the
appalling loss of life which he sees around him daily. Individual
loss, however terrible, can nevertheless be made appreciable
against the wider canvas of the inevitable end of all life – which
is why he comes to realise that his particular experience of the
transcendent, however fleeting and hedged about with sorrow, is
not yet a closing down but the opening up of something else.
Stephen comes to value the idea of his own survival, and the
threads of his life indeed continue after the war in the company
of another Fourmentier, Jeanne, whom he marries in Isabelle's
stead.
War has always been fertile ground for those who want to

explore, against the backdrop of conflict and destruction, the limits of what it means to love in the most challenging and extreme of circumstances. In my last book I mentioned in passing Terrence Malick's film *The Thin Red Line*, which I saw as epitomising the sort of serious engagement with metaphysical issues that I was calling for from the churches.[11] Malick's meditations on love and existence are so powerful that I think they deserve further attention. The film is an adaptation of James Jones' 1963 novel of the same name, which tells the story of a band of soldiers, C-for-Charlie Company, who are attempting to wrest control of Guadalcanal from the Japanese during the south-west Pacific campaign of 1942. Jones' novel is a gritty and often cynical commentary on the realities of modern warfare, and is not sparing of either war's horrors or its absurdities. Men get killed without reason, and there seems no higher logic in why one soldier survives and another does not. But in Malick's hands, a profoundly spiritual dimension enters Jones' implacable universe, since for this film-maker Guadalcanal assumes the characteristics of a sort of paradise lost, where at every turn, in every encounter with the wildlife, or in every meditative reflection on a blade of grass, the fundamental connection between creation and a more meaningful plane of existence is made manifest.

Malick was a professional philosopher before he turned to film-making, and has been influenced, in his equation of nature and spirituality, both by Heidegger and by American transcendentalists like Henry David Thoreau and Ralph Waldo Emerson. The central character of Malick's film, Private Witt (performed by Jim Caviezel in an appropriately enigmatic and elusive way), whose pantheistic viewpoint predominates in the movie, is a visionary with mystical feelings of identification both with his fellow soldiers (as well as the opposing Japanese forces) and with the extraordinary natural world of the jungle which forms the killing fields of his war. As a recent writer has remarked, Witt

> exists comfortably and serenely in nature, and strives to
> actualise the spiritual connection he feels with his fellow
> soldiers as well as the native children of the area and captured
> Japanese men: 'Maybe all men got one big soul,' he muses,
> 'where everybody's a part of it. All faces of the same man, one

big self. Everyone's looking for salvation by themselves. He's like the coal drawn from the fire.'[12]

As this same critic has noted, Witt's reflections on the soul directly echo the first published work of Emerson, *Nature* (1836), which in setting forth the 'manifesto' of transcendentalism stated that 'the universe is composed of nature and the soul', and went on to propose that through communion with nature one could achieve a sort of interpenetrative, communal spirituality.[13] Witt's profound affiliation with nature extends to his love of humanity, and is manifested in particular through his self-sacrifice when he saves his platoon by distracting and leading away a marauding party of Japanese soldiers. The Japanese troops shoot Witt instead of his comrades, and as he dies we see beams of light shining through the trees, as well as images of him swimming, which recapitulate images at the beginning of the film of Witt swimming in the company of the Polynesian islanders. At the end of the film, minutes later, we hear Witt's voice, which seems to be articulating Malick's credo for his whole movie: 'Strife and love, darkness and light. Are they the workings of one mind, features of the same face? Oh my soul, let me be in you now. Look out through my eyes. Look out at the things you made. All things shining.' This almost exactly restates Emerson's own words in another essay called 'The Over-Soul': 'We see the world piece by piece, as the sun, the moon, the animal, the tree; but the whole, of which these are the shining parts, is the soul.'[14] As another recent commentator on the film has noted, it is the paradox of warfare, in Malick's account of it, that it reveals to us 'the radiant splendour of the world and the victory of a faith in spirit'.[15] He comments that 'the final series of shots reveals islanders peacefully paddling canoes up the river, some brightly colored parrots, and then a coconut floating just offshore, sprouting new growth, an emblem of renewal and rebirth, like the shot of the young colt frisking up the river bank that closes John Ford's *Wagonmaster* (1950) as the Mormons cross over into their promised land.'[16] It is the misery of war that reawakens human beings to the question of ultimate Being, which is manifested everywhere – in the laughter of the islanders, in the long and rustling grasses which hide the sinister

threat of snipers' bullets, in the exotic colours of the parrots in
the forest branches – and which reminds them of their mortality,
vulnerability and finitude.[17]

If it is Witt who provides the moral and emotional compass of
the film, perhaps the most interesting and relevant character for
our purposes is Private Bell (played with marvellous and quiet
dignity by the British actor Ben Chaplin). For Bell, it is the
thought of his wife Marty which keeps him afloat during the
hardships of the campaign on Guadalcanal and, in a series of
intense flashbacks (which occur most dramatically and movingly during the key assault on the Japanese positions on the hill
that C-Company has been ordered to capture), he thinks back to
their life together on Hawaii. These dreamlike reminiscences
take on a haunting, visionary quality, complementing the over-
arching pantheistic images within the film as a whole, as well as
the philosophical outlook of Private Witt – and are articulated in
lyrical, overtly metaphysical, terms. We see sensual images
of Bell and his wife back in their Hawaiian home, while
Bell's voice-over proclaims 'We. We together. One being. Flow
together like water. Till I can't tell you from me. I drink you.
Now. Now.' The contrast between the beauty and lyricism of
these scenes and that of the fear, sweat and agony of the soldiers'
assault on Hill 210 is one of the great scenes in contemporary
cinema.

As Malick sees it, war discloses our mortality in a
Heideggerian sense – we are awakened to participation with, or
involvement in, Being through the imminent possibility of death.
This concerns the vital and necessary differentiation between
Being (*Sein*) and beings (*seindes*): 'Being is like an activity in
which all entities are involved and through which they become
present, and this is the sense in which beings participate in
Being. Being is the ground of beings because beings come to
presence through Being.'[18] For Bell, it is through his relationship
with his wife (performed with great sensitivity by Miranda Otto)
that he is awakened, in the midst of battle, to the ground or centre of his being, which discloses the meaning of his life – that he
and Marty are connected, in a way that all creatures are connected, to a reality which is part of and yet transcends their relationship. And yet this connection is not inseparable. Later on, after

the hill has been captured, and C-Company has been granted a week's leave off the line, the mailbags arrive and Bell receives a letter from his wife which tells him that she has fallen in love with an airforce captain and wants a divorce. The letter concludes, in a scene of almost unbearable poignancy, 'We'll meet again someday. People who've been as close as we've been always meet again. I have no right to speak to you this way. I can't stop myself – a habit so strong. Oh, my friend of all those shining years . . . help me leave you.' The intensity of his memories of Marty have sustained Bell in the war, but now abandoned by her he can no longer have access to her presence, even if he survives the next battle to capture Guadalcanal. Nothing in life and love can necessarily be counted on, though the residual power of Bell's recollections of his wife nevertheless instil in him a transcendent sensibility which, like Witt's, sees beyond a world of blood and death to 'blue hills' and 'other shores'.

Perhaps it is in the work of Colin Thubron that the interrelationship of love and memory has, in recent fiction, achieved its fullest and most artistically realised expression. In *Why Bother with Theology?* I tried to show how Thubron's novel *Falling*, although the work of a secular writer, could nevertheless be called profoundly theological and metaphysical in its emphases and proccupations.[19] But his later novel *Turning Back the Sun* arguably dwells even more powerfully than its predecessor on the twin themes of love and loss, articulated through the prism of remembrance. As Thubron tells it, memory is an important facet of who we are as human beings, but must also be treated with care.

The novel's setting is an anonymous town on the edge of the desert, in a new nation that was once a colony, whose inhabitants are all immigrants from elsewhere, 'a conflation of exiles', making up a township that 'belonged to no real community' but who 'cling to the flotsam of a lost security'.[20] Thubron, who is better known as a travel writer than as a novelist, here brings his accomplished forensic powers of descriptive observation to bear on a landscape that is one of the imagination rather than one in which he has actually journeyed. But the result is just as compelling, and conjures a world that seems as touchable and vividly realised as any of his travel memoirs. The power of the novel derives partly from its decision to hold back from contextualising its drama in any place that we might actually identify. The town in which the story unfolds *may* be Alice Springs, just as the un-named fledgling nation *may* be Australia in the period just prior to the Second World War; but no explicit confirmation is made of either possibility. The result of this ambiguity is that the novel, though located in a spatial and temporal setting that we never quite grasp, seems paradoxically more immutable and universal as it assumes the characteristics of an archetype. The world to which Thubron transports us is that of dreams, aspirations, regrets, and above all of memories. Here is a town perched on the edge of nothingness, where 'you can never go back' and where 'the wilderness spreads in a huge, lightless vacancy'.[21] The novel's intensity is extraordinary, and much of this is attributable to the fact that its action unfolds within an inner rather than an outer landscape; indeed, Thubron seems to be as interested in the impact of his fictional topography on the human mind as he is in the landscape itself.

The story is told from the perspective of a man called Rayner, who, like the rest of its inhabitants, is an exile to the town, and is a doctor who has built up a thriving provincial practice there. Rayner, who is described as 'a little awesome' and as exuding a mixture 'of fierceness and sympathy',[22] is exceptional in that, unlike his fellow townspeople, who belong 'here now, or nowhere',[23] he is 'less assimilated than anybody'.[24] Although he expends more energy on the town than 'almost anybody he knew', we learn that 'for all his apparent commitment, his energy, a profound inner betrayal separated him off.'[25] Rayner feels that his life is elsewhere, since he yearns with a bitter longing to return to the capital on the coast, where he grew up, and from which he was separated when he was assigned to work in the town fifteen years before. It emerges that his parents have died, and that there are 'no compassionate grounds for his return there except: *over there is my home*. Which was not enough.'[26] Since later in the book Rayner does return to the capital – and, notwithstanding the temporary permit he has been granted, it seems easy enough for him to do so ('the police stopped him only cursorily, and stamped his residence permit without a question'[27]) – it is tempting to interpret the story metaphorically. The town then comes to represent a state of mind for those who feel themselves to be in some way cut off from the rest of society, or more particularly from what they most love and long for, whatever that may be. It is suggested that the actual mechanics of return – a train journey across the desert – are far less restrictive than the choices and motivations which have led people to end up in what looks like a backwater, emanating claustrophobia and suppressed rage. Thubron's town sits in squat and ugly contradistinction to the 'shimmering city on the coast',[28] which takes on the visionary qualities of an unattainable nirvana, forever tantalising from a distance but frustratingly remaining just out of reach.

Rayner is haunted above all by his recollection of childhood friendships, of a circle of friends who have dispersed, and most particularly of Miriam, with whom he fell in love just before he was transferred from the capital to the desert town. He is tortured by Miriam's memory. Although they never slept together ('the capital was a puritan city'[29]), Rayner remembers in two events the incontestable affirmation of their love. When he is leaving the capital for the last time, his band of friends see him off at the railway station ('their ebullience had shrunk to helplessness. Jarmila and Adelina cried a little, and Leon was biting his lip'[30]), but Miriam was not there:

> Again and again he scrutinised the platform for her. The doors were clunking shut all along the train. The men clasped his hands. Then, at last, he realised that she would not come, and understood. Among this crowd of friends, the gap she had created – her inability to endure this last farewell – was more eloquent than any words she might have spoken.[31]

This, as Rayner sees it, is the first confirmation of her love for him. The second is to be found in another memory, that of an occasion just prior to his departure, and following shortly on from a car accident in which his mother was killed and his foot was twisted and permanently injured. We learn that he and Miriam used to go diving west of the capital on the coral coast, and after his discharge from hospital he takes the trip with Miriam and his friends once more. But his disfigurement now

means that he cannot fit his injured foot into a flipper. So he
follows Miriam overboard, 'furious with humiliation' and
'barefoot':

> Rayner did not know it then, but this would be the last time he
> would see her. He felt a little sick. The rasp of a strong current
> clouded the water with a dust of coral fragments. Miriam
> swam ahead of him with languid undulations of her flippered
> feet. The compressed-air cylinders obscured her back. All
> familiarity seemed gone from her, because she had dyed her
> dark hair pale – a smoky gold colour, which flowed out behind
> her. Even when she turned, her face floated enigmatic behind
> its mask and regulator, washed by this flaxen strangeness.
>   He came alongside her with strenuous thrusts of his
> unaided feet. The others were ahead, oblivious of them. The
> current had eased now, and the water cleared. In a dreamy
> unison they glided together abreast, as if flying, while the coral
> steepened into miniature crags around them.
>   Then came the moment by which he remembered their love.
> He reached out and took her hand. Behind its mask her face
> looked startled for a moment, then she pulled his hand
> towards her and held it clenched against her breast. The next
> instant, teasingly, she had taken the regulator out of her mouth
> and was holding it towards him. So he removed his own and
> gave it to her, and childishly, a little dangerously, breathing
> from each other's cylinders, they swam on for a full two
> minutes, locked side by side. It was a moment of perfect trust.
> They went in slow motion, weightless. They might have been
> breathing through each other's lungs. She still clasped his
> hand. They must have looked like one creature, he later
> thought – but an inept mutant, doomed to perish. Yet it was an
> instant of such eerie, unaccountable union that he imagined it
> afterwards more complete than the sexual coupling they had
> never known, and as if to illumine the moment's strangeness,
> great drifts of damsel-fish, confined in the coral valley, came
> flickering and brushing against them like cold gems.[32]

Rayner's frustration at his sense of loss, both of Miriam and of
the capital which contained their love, is manifested in his sub-

sequent relationships with women, which are conducted 'in the
knowledge that one day he would leave . . . his commitment was
to somewhere else.'[33] These substitute love affairs are characterised most of all by 'the knowledge of their transience', even
though several of the women 'had come to love him, as he cooled
towards them'.[34] Yet this fickleness changes when he meets a
dancer called Zoë, who, like Rayner, is an exile from the city, but
who, unlike him, seems to feel no deep allegiance to anything
now but her art. Zoë is an amalgam of contradictions, whose
character 'splinters with awesome complexity',[35] and whose
fundamental mystery is manifested in 'sudden fervours and
withdrawals'.[36] She comes to fascinate Rayner, who – despite
himself – is drawn to her passion, her unpredictability, and her
fierce vitality, which manifests itself in everything that she is and
does. When he first sees her perform, Rayner recognises that her
dancing is not an affectation, or assumption of some other role
(temporarily put on for the entertainment of the club's punters,
who feel repelled and angered by Zoë's 'inacessibility'[37]) but an
expression of who she is: a manifestation of her inner essence:

> She released herself headlong into the music. Her dancing was
> as she'd said, an amalgam of her own: a tumult of twisting,
> leaping and mime, out of which – as if from early training –
> erupted balletic pirouettes and arabesques. She seemed to
> dance out of some defiant core in her, without thought of her
> audience. The music throbbed and swung. Every movement
> shouted: this is *me*! Even her figure, encased in a vulgar
> iridescent leotard, came as a surprise. Her torso with its long,
> delicate arms and soft-looking breasts, descended to full hips
> and strong dancer's legs. She seemed less sexual than
> violently, daemonically physical.[38]

Rayner feels torn by his love for this vibrant, vital woman,
whose exuberance and naturalness so mesmorise and fascinate
him, and his desire to return to the capital. Yet he feels sure that,
whatever temporary relief and solace Zoë might bring him,
fulfilment lies elsewhere. A letter from his aunt arrives, which
indicates that she has only months to live, and that she intends
for Rayner to inherit her house in the capital. Arrangements have

been made, and a permit authorised, for him to visit. She inti-
mates also that there is a practice in the city which is seeking a
junior partner, and that she has mentioned Rayner's name in this
connection. Should he accept the position, she believes that 'the
indefinite extension of his permit would be only a formality'.[39] It
seems that all is ready for Rayner to fulfil his dream and return
to the life from which he has felt torn, and for which he has
yearned, for so many years. In an agony of loss, which wells 'up
inside him like nausea',[40] he tells Zoë of his impending departure
from the town, which he expects will be for ever:

> She said in a brimming voice, 'Did you always know you'd
> leave me?'
>   'Yes.' The moment he said this he realised that it wasn't
> quite true, but it seemed better not to tell her now.
>   'That must have been strange.'
>   Yes, he thought, strange and terrible. Yet while you were
> living the relationship, even with the prospect of eventual
> betrayal, it seemed natural. But he could not explain to her this
> waiting to return, this knowledge that completeness lay
> somewhere else.[41]

On his return to the city, Rayner initially finds that his
memories have held true. The terraced and balconied mansions
that he remembers, 'with their white-washed pediments and
frail lunettes above the doors'[42] transport him 'in a euphoria of
recognition'[43] to an adolescent world epitomised by the street
of his parents' house, whose 'balconies and verandahs frothed
with wrought iron',[44] and a garden of roses and jasmine, whose
'mingled scent, sharp with the tang of the distant sea, was the
fragrance of his childhood'.[45] However, his later conversations
with his aunt Birgit, which put a different complexion on his
reminiscences, and a meeting with his old friend Leon, followed
by a reunion with Miriam, force him to recognise how little he
had understood of any of his and his friends' childhoods.[46] Leon,
who has been in and out of psychiatric hospitals, seems stuck in
his childhood memories, and unable to move on. His attach-
ments and preoccupations are fundamentally underdeveloped
and infantile:

He recalled picnics, balls and bathing parties, teenage jokes and childish vendettas, abortive loves, clandestine boating expeditions, accidents, all in a tapestry of detail. Rayner could not remember half of them. But to Leon the act of remembering had attained a terrible, all-absorbing meaning. His anecdotes followed one another in a maudlin rush, and the old, fastidious intelligence which Rayner remembered was powerless against it.[47]

Leon's state of arrested development is traced back to an incident in their childhoods that Rayner suddenly recollects, when he, Leon and their other friends, Gerhard and Ivar, had caught a lizard beneath a balustrade, and were deciding whether or not to release or 'execute' it. After much childish discussion and debate, the boys decide to let the gecko go. But though Leon is 'squeamish' and apparently accedes to this verdict, he is, we are told, 'in the grip of a secret excitement'.[48] Growing bored, the boys drift away, and sit exhausted in the sun, but after a while Ivar and Rayner are roused from their lassitude by a 'dry, violent pounding'.[49] The sight which they see is altogether private and inexplicable: 'beneath them, with cold, frenzied blows of the rock, Leon was pulping the lizard to death.'[50] This disturbing recollection sets in motion Rayner's reappraisal of his situation and motivations. He comes to understand that he has been living a dream, that the behaviour of his friends was not always what it seemed, and that memories can be deceptive and misleading. The more that he experiences it in reality, the more that the city seems to fade, and his memories begin to thin and disperse like mist. The capital lacks the vitality both of Zoë and of the town which he has dismissed and rejected: it is missing some essential quality of *definition*, so that, like the gaze of its inhabitants, it begins to drift away from him:

> During his last few days, Rayner took to rambling the city
> streets and parks . . . Occasionally, a little way in front of him,
> he imagined he recognised the rangy stride of Adelina or the
> froth of Miriam's curls. But when he drew alongside, the
> expression which met his would be blank. In fact he saw
> nobody he knew. And people seemed to move in a languid

self-absorption. Their eyes might meet his, but they rarely
focused, and he came to associate this dreamy stare with the
city: a gaze without penetration, like the becalmed vision of a
cat. Whole shops and restaurants and streets were filled with
it. It turned them faintly unreal. Even the young women,
looking back at him, would only glance away or smile after
two or three seconds. A few of them were beautiful. But most
looked merely pretty, like mezzotints. He could not imagine
them losing their tempers or making love. They only made
him ache for Zoë: her exuberance and irreverence and
unpredictable passions.[51]

Realising at last that he wants to 'go home',[52] and that home is
to be found in the rough and ready, rumbustious character of the
town, Rayner declines the position offered him in the city's medical practice. His 'conversion' is complete upon finally meeting
Miriam. His childhood sweetheart has married and divorced,
and has a daughter. At first she seems just as Rayner remembered her ('He might have opened a door onto the past . . . She
stood there in a white dress. The same dark eyes were smiling at
him from her brown face. The familiar curls shifted around her
shoulders. The same brimming figure radiated health'[53]). But the
recollections on which he has built his hopes soon come tum-
bling down. In their conversation, Miriam reveals both that,
while diving, she once shared a regulator with Gerhard,[54] making
a mockery of any special regard she might have had for Rayner,
and that the reason she did not see Rayner off at the station years
before was because she was attending 'somebody's twenty-first
birthday', and couldn't come.[55] Rayner realises, even as the tears
prick his eyes as he embraces her, that he has invested the memory of Miriam with a forcefulness and significance which her real
personality shows to be unwarranted.

And so Rayner makes his way back to the frontier town, which
has been tormented for months both by drought and by a rising
hysteria attendant upon the random killings of its inhabitants,
seemingly by the aboriginal peoples of the desert. A disease has
broken out, which is manifested in a rash that seems to appear
without medical cause or premonition, and which is attributed
to contact, sexual or otherwise, with the so-called 'savages', or

aboriginals. Zoë has already contracted the disease, whose real provenance and effects are unknown, and which also has no known antidote. As he leaves the city, Rayner too has felt the tell-tale mark of the virus:

> The water covered his back in tepid bursts. He soaped it idly. Then, as he glanced down at his body, he saw the blemish slapped on it like a leech. It dribbled blackly from one nipple amost to his groin. It had erupted without warning, overnight.
> He froze, waiting. Yet he was not struck by disgust, or fear, or even surprise. He touched it tentatively with his fingertips, in recognition. Its chocolate snake gleamed between the runnels of soap. It smeared his ribs like the dirt of reality. It seemed less like a recent eruption than an awesome birthmark. He let the water trickle over it, skirting sometimes its raised roughness, and remembered it on Zoë's body, and on a hundred others.[56]

The mark of the disease resembles the character of the wilder-ness itself, which, like Zoë and the natives, defies easy categori-sation or simplistic attribution. It is the wilderness which gives the town its atavistic, primeval energy, and which turns it inwards in order to protect itself against a 'distant apprehension of peril':[57]

> Of course you couldn't exclude that wilderness. The vista at the end of most streets was closed by a low, unbreaking wave of violet hills. Blood-coloured crags and ridges surged along the northern suburbs and burst up even in the town's heart. On the outskirts, two-lane roads stopped dead, petering into tracks or stones. Between habitation and desert was only a step.[58]

Thubron implies that – despite Rayner's memories of the chimerical city he feels he has lost – those who, like Zoë and Rayner, move to the town in fact become inseparably connected to something else altogether: to a 'mysterious, uninscribed land, ancient and empty' and an 'antique country, which seemed to promise nothing beyond itself'.[59] Something about the

wilderness infects them, and literally gets under their skin. The
land, and the natives who inhabit it, have a character that is in
the end implacable and mysterious. The disease which afflicts
the town's inhabitants, and which may or may not have a connection with the natives, is as inexplicable as the nature of the
country itself. This is a land that defies any attempts to label or
tame it, which is why Zoë – and, in the end, Rayner – are so
much better suited to its environment than the insipid environs
of the capital, whose citizens seem by turns complacent, frivo-
lous and indistinct. Rayner comes to understand that he needs
the inexplicability and raw power of this world to a far greater
degree than the 'civilized' and sophisticated coastal city of his
remembrance. His empathy for the wilderness is manifested in
his sympathetic attitude to the natives, which goes very much
against the grain of the white man's consensus. He refuses to
sign a fabricated notification of death, when a native has died
under duress from the military, and he and Zoë give temporary
lodging to an old aboriginal and his young daughter, despite the
opprobrium contingent upon such an act, and their probable
censure should the refugees be discovered. This is a passionate,
dangerous and unpredictable place. When the water-holes are
empty, the natives have been known to 'dry out . . . in the head'[60]
and go on a killing spree. But this comes to seem nothing so
much as the activity of a people 'coeval with all this violent,
ancient land – a people to whom death was only the flow of time
and of the clan'.[61]

Rayner's childhood friend Ivar – the only one of their band to
have ended up with him in the town – is now a military com-
mander. Unlike Rayner, Ivar seems to see in the volatile, frontier
mentality of the town his route to self-advancement, and in this
lies their essential separation. While Ivar recognises the radical
distinctiveness of the aboriginals, he sees them – with the repel-
lent and dispassionate logic of a convinced social Darwinist –
solely as a threat to be eliminated: 'These people are radically
different,' he tells Rayner at one point. 'You only have to look at
their heads to see it. There simply isn't enough room for a developed neo-cortex.'[62] Rayner and Zoë stand in opposition to such a
position – a sort of rationalistic, deterministic fundamentalism –
and represent in the novel the compassionate and more human

desire to embrace difference and diversity without passing judgement. It is fitting that Rayner returns to the town for good, and in doing so requests Zoë's forgiveness for his desertion. At the end of the novel, the idea that this is a mysterious and unaccountable world, whose character resists analysis or interpretation, is reaffirmed. Suborned for military duty by Ivar – as a punishment, Rayner feels, for his earlier refusal to sign a military certificate for the aboriginal's death – Rayner drives out into the wilderness with his old friend and an accompanying party of soldiers, to try to locate a native war party. What the expedition discovers in the desert is something it could never have bargained for. Stumbling at last upon a band of natives, who are advancing along a rock outcrop towards the edge of a sheer drop, the soldiers are able to witness a ritual imbued with all the mystery and power of the desert land itself:

> Rayner stared back across the chasm, with sweat dripping into his eyes. He could make out the painted countenances on the natives' shields now and the jostling, whitened faces above them, and the feathered tassels on the ceremonial thongs. As he watched, the natives' dancing trembled to a halt at the edge of the drop. Nothing intervened now between them and the sun. Their keening rose to a heart-breaking crescendo, and some of them lifted long, cylindrical wooden horns to their mouths, like monstrous bassoons, which blared and moaned under the chanting.
>
> All round Rayner the soldiers were standing up in full view and gazing across the chasm, uncomprehending. Their rifles strewed the rocks. The sun burnished the earth round them and lit their astonished faces. Some of them sat speechless on the boulders. The sergeant, who had just noticed the women crowded along the ridge behind, kept muttering, 'What's happening here? What the hell's happening?'
>
> By now, at the headland's end, the savages were massed in a coppery glow of bodies, their shields fallen to their sides. As the sun touched the skyline, the singing and the bray of horns quickened with pathetic urgency, Rayner felt a foolish grief for them. Their sounds intertwined in a wavering threnody, which echoed less like the prayer of humans than the mourning of

some unearthly animal. Perhaps it was a distortion of the atmosphere which delayed the sun on the wilderness' rim. But for an instant – so Rayner thought – its red circle and the sharp-edged clouds froze in the sky.

Then inexorably, yet half against his expectation, the sun was halved, then quartered, by the black edge of the wilderness, then disappeared.

At first, while scarlet clouds littered the sky, all the force of the chanting continued. Then, in slow groups of two or three, the natives began to disperse back over the promontory, and the sounds broke up and faded away. Momentarily, from the point where the sun had vanished, there radiated upwards an enigmatic flush, as if a furnace had been lit just beneath the horizon. Then this too retreated, and left only a pallor over the desert.[63]

In their attempts to 'turn back the sun' – to restore a harmony to creation and human society that they feel has been lost, when a mythical tree was felled at the centre of their world – the aboriginals are seemingly in touch with secret powers which the whites, for all their racial hubris and superior 'civilization', feel that they have lost, and by which they are awed and humbled. The message of *Turning Back the Sun* is that there is an unaccountability at the centre of existence which cannot be defined or easily made rational. In fact, rationality of the sort which gives Ivar his complacent and chilling self-assurance – and which in his view legitimates ethnic cleansing, so that one race makes way for another – is precisely the kind which Thubron signals as being maleficent, reprehensible and to be condemned. It is no coincidence that as the war party makes its way back to the town, the skies fill with rain clouds for the first time in months, auguring the end of the drought and native marauding. Deep magic has been performed, and the elements have responded and been harmonised.

The love that Rayner has for Zoë emerges as being of a more lasting and tangible sort than any pseudo-love which Rayner believes that he has for the capital and what it represents, most particularly in the person of Miriam. While memory, as we have seen, can carry our worlds, and help us to discover who we are, it is important to be alert to the limitations and Circean pitfalls of recollection. Memories can be deceptive. When they help to perpetuate a notion of superiority, or separateness, which is at odds with the reality of shared human companionship conducted in the face of inevitable loss and suffering, they offer us a false trail, and reveal the outlines merely of a mirage, whose contours fade away in the heat of the day. Thubron's humanity and deep sensitivity towards other people and cultures – which is evident throughout his entire oeuvre of travel writing – is articulated here in his most passionate and compassionate novel. He shows that it is possible for love to endure against the odds, since Rayner returns to the town, having renounced his former obsession, and desires nothing more than to be reunited with Zoë. He shows that people are most themselves when they cultivate a sense of integration with their environment, with a land which is not theirs to exploit, or 'control' by attempted genocide, but which is held in custodianship, while yet being integrated with something altogether 'bigger' and more significant than their individual selves. Finally, he shows that 'meaning' is not necessarily 'graspable' and may remain inaccessible – as it is in a mysterious blemish of the skin, or in the natives' attempt, in their secret ceremony, to restore balance to the created order. While their ritual may seem 'irrational' (at least in any sense that Ivar might understand it), it is yet deeply impressive and moving, to the degree that even the soldiers are stunned into a sense of immobility and reverence.

'Love', at least in Thubron's lexicon, can therefore be understood as love of the apparently ordinary and commonplace, whether it be a physical deformity, of white skin or black, or of a day-to-day relationship which is not conducted in any terms which might be understood as 'glamorous' or falsely nostalgic, but which in its very immediacy and vitality can effect moral and emotional transformation. Rayner's love for Zoë, which is based on their mutual rejection of a culture which strives for control – of the natives, of the land, of what should and shouldn't be performed in Zoë's club – is more lasting and significant than any deceptive ennui or desire for domination. In their relationship with each other, and in Rayner's awakening sense that he is connected to the wilderness (which up to the point of his return he

had rejected in favour of a civilisation which has no real understanding of the landscape it has 'colonised'), we sense that it is
within the very ordinariness and familiarity of things that we
may discern the epiphanic and the extraordinary. Through an
openness to the mysterious wonders of the earth's ancient landscape, and an attempt to understand these, rather than manipu-
late them to our own ends, we may glimpse something which
exists beyond it – the transcendent – which confers 'meaning' on
our lives, and which enables us to live harmoniously and lovingly with one another.

   In this chapter I have explored various secular accounts of
how love might be understood, and how love interacts with
memory. Such accounts are stories which tell us that our lives
have 'meaning'. What I have tried to show is that our remembrance of love, like our remembrance of loss, is a way of binding
ourselves to the world and to what we hold most cherishable.
Memory confers meaning on our present lives and enables continuity with both past and future. In our memories lies wisdom.
At the same time, I have tried to indicate that recollection –
which has emerged as a key theme in the book – must be treated
with care and with an appropriate degree of hermeneutical suspicion. It is not just in memory – which can sidetrack us, or lure
us from where we really need to go – that we discover who we
are, but in the current, vital process of living in, and interacting
with, the present-day encounters which bring us face to face
with our experience of the transcendent. Such encounters may
seem workaday and uninspiring. They may seem closed to any
sort of higher 'truth'. God may often seem far away, or inaccessible through prayer or meditation. But I believe that it is precisely in such meetings – those day-to-day relationships with
other human beings in which we work out our essential humanity – wherein our meaning and purpose are to be divulged. Love,
whether between individuals, or countries, or cultures, is at the
heart of our divine calling to be human. So often we mess things
up. So often we fail to be open to the possibility of change and
transformation. But in opening ourselves to the other, which is
also the Other, we change not just ourselves, but the world of
which we are all part. Such opening up also means letting go –
of our securities, self-confidences and self-protective assurances.

Gain and loss; loss and gain. But in letting go of self-love, of the desire to dominate, so often we find that we are loved. And therein lies fulfilment and the true 'meaning' of our lives. In the next chapter I want to turn to the nature of such fulfilment, and ask of what it might be said to consist.

CHAPTER 4

Fulfilment

My name, and yours, and the true name of the sun, or a spring of water, or an unborn child, are all syllables of the great word that is very slowly spoken by the shining of the stars. There is no other power, no other name . . . For a word to be spoken, there must be silence. Before, and after.

Ursula Le Guin, from *The Farthest Shore*

They sat them down upon the yellow sand,
Between the sun and moon upon the shore;
And sweet it was to dream of Fatherland,
Of child, and wife, and slave; but evermore
Most weary seem'd the sea, weary the oar,
Weary the wandering fields of barren foam.
Then some one said, 'We will return no more;'
And all at once they sang, 'Our island home
Is far beyond the wave; we will no longer roam.'

Tennyson, from *The Lotos-Eaters*

In a year, light travels six million million miles.

It flies from the sun to the earth in eight minutes. It crosses the whole solar system in eleven hours.

Light flies to the nearest star in our galaxy, Alpha Centauri, in four cold dazzling years. But there are several hundred thousand million stars in our galaxy.

After eighty thousand years of travel through interstellar gas and dust and stars, light has crossed the galaxy. But it is only one galaxy among unimaginably many. Light from at least one hundred thousand million galaxies is travelling towards us, through us, beyond us.

The whole observable universe would take thousands of millions of years for light to cross. But a single year is a very long time to us; see how far the light has gone already.

Maggie Gee, from *Light Years*

Basingstoke – Winchester – Cambridge – East Oxford – East London – Islington – Malvern – Berkhamsted – Bayswater. The waymarks of a life, they skid past my gaze like stations viewed momentarily through the window of a careering and clattering train. Each stop has its own commuters, with their own preoccupations, aspirations and dreams. Recognisably connected – yet altogether distinct – lives inhabit the places where once mine too was lived. Who walks, I wonder, where I once walked? Whose hearts are broken where once mine too was beaten and cracked? Who searches there – in the grimy racks of that obscure shop under the railway arch – for the rare and collectable records that I used to covet? Who sits conversing now on the worn-away steps of the market cross, as I once did, and as did countless lives before mine, way back to a medieval century? Whose feet tread now in my vanished footsteps, and whose talk is heard in the streets of the town where my childhood came of age and expired? Life feels like it's lived in a station which I am always leaving. Faces and features I knew slide by on the platform like a jumble of signs on the highway. What's left on the journey are memories. Sad, extraordinary, painful, hopeful, transient, lasting – paradoxical – they pass away down the tracks, or, like so many twigs, are carried downriver to an unguessable end.

For years I came to Norfolk. Come weekends, I'd pile into the car with friends, or girlfriends, and head north. Away from the grime and grind. I wanted to feel connected to something bigger – huger – than my own concerns. That's why I drove up to Holkham: an epic, lung-bursting landscape of sand, sky and a turquoise sea that you had to walk miles to reach, glittering in the sunlit distance like a lambent jewel. The years went by. Friends and lovers came and went. Life continued its wayward course, meandering mazily like the haphazard

trails of the lugworms in north Norfolk's grainy sand. But while the
days shapeshifted and teased, Holkham beach was always special, too
important to change too much – immutable, reliable, ageless. Out there
on the rainwashed tide, the debris of other people's lives came floating
by. I picked up old shoes, boots, children's jackets, discarded pictures:
the melancholy detritus of abandonment and loss. Out there, behind the
horizon, was an answer to all these offloaded questions – but a solution
hidden now by the sighing flow-ebb-flow of time and history. I come to
Holkham still, drawn by its limitless horizon, that supernatural space
between once and once again. And it's out there – there, beside the
snarling tideline, pungent with the whiff of fish and salt, that I think I
can see something else. My heart seems to swell, as the waves snap at
my shoeless feet, the gulls scream into the wind and I look out over the
North Sea, which races over the beach in roaring surges. Filled with a
euphoria of longing, it's then that I want to reach out and embrace it
all: time and tides, lost lovers and friends, the peerless darkening sky,
and all creation.

'All creation.' Spiritualities which focus just on self-realisation or
the actualisation of the individual so often overlook that vital
communal component. We are all connected to something larger
than ourselves, which binds us to it, to the world, and to each
other. As Terrence Malick, drawing on the philosophy of
Heidegger, so movingly shows in his film *The Thin Red Line*,
beings are the extension of Being, but need to recover their sense
of pantheistic connectedness to Being in order to be truly themselves. The paradox of being separate beings is that we are all
part of a larger, transcendent Being which yet confers meaning
and distinctiveness on our individuality. I have little time, therefore, for people who talk about spirituality as if it were something that relates just to themselves, their own processes of
enlightenment, or their own interests. To talk about 'meaning' as
it affects the self is to talk about the meaning of the world and of
our neighbours and companions on life's road. We cannot get
away from the fact that we are social creatures, whose existence
is oriented towards one another, and whose purpose is acted out
in concert with others. The personal is merely the precursor to
the political. When we talk about 'fulfilment', therefore, we need
to keep in mind what has been one of the foci of this book

throughout: that self and world cannot be separated in any truly meaningful way, and that what we do as individuals in the world has a direct impact on the lives of our fellows as well as on the environment which nourishes and supports us all. We all have a duty to world and neighbour, since our neighbours are fellow custodians of a planet that we have on trust until we die, and because we are bound together under the terms of a relationship which affects us universally. Of course not all people in our lifetimes will appreciate the ramifications of this connectedness in the same way, and many of us – especially in the West – appear to have forgotten what it means to treat the earth and its raw materials with respect and reverence. Our dependency on the accumulation of capital, and on the consumption which fuels our market economies, leads always more certainly towards a system that rewards some more than it does others, while it is those 'others' (the poor, the marginalised, the excluded) who feel pushed ever further outwards to the margins of self-respect and sustainability.

As Rowan Williams has noted recently, the forces of globalisation have involved Westerners in a 'Faustian contract', which has involved us in 'dramas we never thought of . . . roles we never chose'.[1] As Williams says, we want access to the goods that unrestricted markets will bring, but we have yet to understand what the greater part of humanity sees as the corollary of this: that 'the prosperous will be seen as the makers of poverty. In the global village, the one who becomes rich is seen as the thief of his neighbour's goods.'[2] The consequence of such inequality of influence is that we in the West have a life 'in other people's imagination, quite beyond our control'[3] – to the degree that the disenfranchised and bitter, the bin Ladens, the Mohammad Attas and the Madrid bombers, quite probably see in the golden arches of McDonalds (let alone the Twin Towers) straddling cities from Algiers to Antananarivo, all the incentive that they need to tear down what such symbols seem to represent: the economic and cultural hegemony of an exploitative and unjust geopolitical ideology. When we talk about 'meaning', therefore, we need to keep in mind what socio-economic conditions underlie such a discussion. When we try to assess the value of different kinds of 'spirituality', are we including in that assessment those

whose voices might be muffled or even silenced, or whose priorities are not so much 'finding themselves' as finding enough
water and food to survive into the next day? Or the security to
live in their own homes, free from fear or oppression, with the
capacity to exercise an appropriate degree of self-determination
to enable their basic human flourishing? The focus on the self
that so often forms the bedrock of alternative Western spiritualities has an unattractively self-indulgent dimension to it, and its
lack of cosmological responsibility or interest in social justice, are
only made possible through a circumstantial disjuncture of economic and political power.

Any discussion of 'fulfilment' as a cornerstone of human
'meaning' has therefore to keep in mind just who it is who is
being fulfilled. The few, or the many? The black or the white?
The gay or the straight? The rich or the poor? The powerful or
the disenfranchised? The oppressed or the oppressor? In considering the facets and manifestations of all creation, we should
dwell on the plurality of the world that we inhabit as tenants. If
human beings are made in the image of God, as the great religious traditions of Islam, Christianity and Judaism would have
it, then all people – not just some – are repositories of a divine
spark and are worthy of reverence and respectful reciprocity.
Cultural and ethnic diversity should be welcomed in our world,
and embraced joyfully as a means to understand not only one
another but also ourselves. For when we look into the eyes of the
other, whether those eyes are blue or brown or black, we look out
at another facet of the Creator who gives us light and life and fills
our own selves with meaning and purpose and grace. A society
which closes itself to difference, which shuns plurality, is turning
inwards and shutting itself off from the energy by which it may
mature and develop in future. It chooses sterility over succour,
barrenness over creativity, and prejudice and selfishness over
generosity and hope. Our world is filled to its brim with vibrant
colour and with the rich spectacle of millions of species, both
plant and animal, which dazzle us with their complexity and
wondrous diversity. An appropriate meditation on natural life
ought to lead us to an understanding, then, that the glory of
creation lies not in its uniformity but its pluriformity. Creation is
sacrosanct. Acts of environmental despoliation ought to be as

sacrilegious and grossly offensive to our sensibilities as racism and economic injustice. To be properly 'fulfilled' is to look towards the attainment of a world where exploitation, in all its forms, is combated and condemned. In the angry chatter of the twenty-first century, within a world dominated by ethnic suspicion and intercultural recrimination, we need increasingly to take heed of the words of religious visionaries like Govind Singh, who wrote these inspiring and irenic words four hundred years ago:

Lord! Thou art the Hindu, the Muslim, the Turk and the Feringhi;
Thou art the Persian, the Sanskritian, the Arabian;
Thou art the speech . . . Thou art the warrior clad in shining
   armour, and thou art the peace supreme!
Thou art man, woman, child and God!
Thou art the flute player, the herdsman that goes grazing his dumb cows!
Thou bestoweth love and thou givest thyself to all!
Thou art the protector of life and the giver of all prosperity!
Thou art the cure of all sorrow and suffering.
In all shapes and everywhere, thou art dear to me;
In every form thou art myself!
Thou art my vow . . . my beginning and my end.[4]

I have deliberately entitled his chapter 'fulfilment' rather than 'happiness', because the modern notion of the latter is intrinsically bound up with post-Enlightenment ideas of human autonomy and freedom which have not always been as liberating or as helpful as they sometimes profess to be. 'Happiness' is an elusive concept, but it is dependent on the assumption that people are in some fundamental way architects of their own destinies and futures. This concept of radical self-determination contrasts markedly with antiquity's notion of the pursuit of the good life, which in the ancient world was integrally related to virtue, and therefore to the idea that personal fulfilment could only be manifested in harmony with the lives of one's fellow citizens – and specifically in, as Ziyad Marar puts it, 'the moral standards to which we can appeal in guiding our interactions with the world'.[5] The tension between the questions 'what do I really want?' and 'how ought I to live?' is thus the tension between an

archaic and a relatively contemporary way of conceptualising
the world, and it is a tension which makes the concept of happiness both remarkably fundamental to our notions of a complete
and well-rounded individuality, as well as incredibly hard to
define or fathom. The idea located in much of Western thought
that we have a divine right to happiness (a right which is
enshrined, for example, in the American constitution, and which
is often taken as the benchmark of modern democratic thinking)
has frequently had a baleful effect on the lives of those who are
seen to get in the way of such happiness's realisation. If the idea
of happiness is cut loose from society more broadly, and is seen
to relate not to the moral imperatives of our companions, or to
how we improve the lot of the needy and suffering, but rather to
our own self-actualisation, then it is not hard to see how aspirations towards our 'completion' as human beings could be seen to
be threatened by the similar aspirations of others. The primacy of
the self fails to find room for the collaborative development and
moral improvement of the world. It is for this reason that I find
the idea of 'fulfilment' more apposite, as well as more fruitful
and helpful, than the notion of 'happiness' as a central category
for defining human 'meaning'.

The concept of fulfilment enables us to see that our individu-
alised 'meanings' as human beings ought to be closely related to
the 'meanings' of the world that contains us – as well as to the
complementary lives and 'meanings' of the people who co-
inhabit our planet. It also enables us to begin to look at human
completion according to a time frame that extends beyond the
immediate and shallow vistas of instant self-gratification. The
capitalist imperative drives us ever onwards to acquire more in
the way of 'stuff', and is so powerful a force in our society that it
overflows, as we have seen, into how we view our own relationships, which so often now are reduced to a sort of commodification of exchange. True fulfilment, as Ursula Le Guin suggests
in her science fiction novel *The Dispossessed*, is a more elusive and
yet ultimately more rewarding goal than transient pleasure or
superficial acquisitiveness. For as one of her characters, Shevek,
reflects in the book, 'If you evade suffering, you also evade the
chance of joy. Pleasure you may get, or pleasures, but you will
not be fulfilled. You will not know what it is to come home.'[6] Le

Guin's brilliantly drawn character Shevek is a temporal physicist attempting to reconcile the politically estranged inhabitants of the planets Anarres and Urras by working out an amazing scientific theorem called the 'principle of simultaneity' – a theorem which will revolutionise interstellar communication and commerce throughout his galaxy.[7] But as he undergoes many vicissitudes and struggles in the process of completing his life's work, and as the elusive theorem hovers frustratingly at the edge of his consciousness, Shevek reflects at one point – in a way that reflects Le Guin's own Taoist philosophy – that 'fulfilment is a function of time':

> The search for pleasure is circular, repetitive, atemporal. The variety-seeking of the spectator, the thrill-hunter, the sexually-promiscuous, always ends in the same place. It has an end. It comes to the end and has to start over. It is not a journey and return, but a closed cycle, a locked room, a cell . . . It is not until an act occurs within the landscape of the past and the future that it is a human act. Loyalty, which asserts the continuity of past and future, binding time into a whole, is the root of human strength; there is no good to be done without it . . . So, looking back on the last four years, Shevek saw them not as wasted, but as part of the edifice that he and Takver were building with their lives. The thing about working with time, instead of against it, he thought, is that it is not wasted. Even pain counts.[8]

Le Guin's notion that the meaning of life is to be found in such common or garden virtues as human loyalty, which binds time together and helps us to construct lasting structures for our lives, enables her to adopt a cosmic perspective on ethics and morality which is articulated through more than just the science fiction settings of many of her novels. She is able, again and again, to express an attractively empathic understanding of all her characters, and of the diverse worlds they inhabit – however marked these people's individual flaws and failings may be – because she understands with great sensitivity and compassion that compromise and suffering are part and parcel of being human. People are here to stick together, whether through good times and bad, famine or plenty, sorrow or joy; and as she sees it, the yardstick of how we measure up as human beings depends on how we conduct our relationships with others and on the altruism we exercise within society as a whole.

The idea that true fulfilment comes to those who wait was one that I reflected on day after day, as I trudged over the Malvern hills during the Babylonian exile that was my summer of unemployment, and as the prospect of an ongoing fifteen-year career seemed to be evaporating as certainly as the early morning mist on the fell-tops. As a publisher I had already learned to adopt a long-term game-plan. One cannot afford to do otherwise, when building a list takes years rather than days or months to bring about, and when commissioning a book, waiting for an author to write and deliver it, and then steering it through the production process, all have to be factored into the overall publishing process. Anyone, employer or employee, who looks for instant gratification in a publishing role, and who prioritises short-termism at the expense of a mature, phlegmatic process of things eventually coming to fruition, is sure to end up disappointed. Thus, when my job was taken from me, I did have some underlying sense of what digging in for the long haul was likely to entail: grit, determination, and a tiring but perhaps ultimately rewarding hike to the summit. But there was something about the landscape itself, some sensibility of the Malverns' immense geological and geophysical history, which reinforced my feeling that fulfilment should be seen in its proper perspective. Le Guin's cosmic preoccupations – and in the context of her novels, human life unfolds most meaningfully when it is considered against a wide canvas of planets and stars – make greater sense when one considers the humbling geological forces that have shaped our own world, beside whose titanic pressures and immense geophysical powers our own lives are rendered miniscule and insignificant. We have already seen, in Chapter 1, how our ancestors viewed the natural world as more than just a landscape; it was the gateway to a magical internal topography which was populated by invisible spirits and powers, and fuelled by the energies of the imagination. Brian Bates reminds us that

In any area where human perception, consciousness and emotions interact with non-human factors, simple scientific descriptions in the physical sense are inadequate. Intuitive language and imaginative images can better describe a myriad of subtle factors. For our ancestors, the imagination was the doorway from the everyday to the Otherworld. And there was a constant flowing of the imagination into the material world. The sense of reality in Middle-earth was more an awareness of realities, in the plural.[9]

By acknowledging that scientific, rational enquiry has limits in how it can explain the world, and by reconnecting with the power of the imagination, as this is expressed through myth and story, we are able to bring a perspective to bear on the natural landscape which offers much more than just intellectual embroidering. Le Guin, for one, stands solidly in this pastoral story-telling tradition, as novels of hers like *The Farthest Shore*, *The Dispossessed* and *City of Illusions* eloquently testify, since all, to a greater or lesser degree, reflect with meditative intensity on the energising power of landscape.[10] A deeper, more reflective perspective on the life of the natural world tells us something rather important about the character of fulfilment. We need an adequate sense of proportion, which is why Maggie Gee's cosmological reflections in her novel *Light Years* are so apposite and helpful. At one point she writes there that

The earth will go on circling the sun for another five thousand million years. Then the sun will slowly expand and redden, the earth will be drawn, with Venus and Mercury, into a new red giant star, and the star will pulsate and shoot most of its contents out across the emptiness. They will hang on the dark, the ghost of the sun, a red-blue ring of gas and dust . . . In billions of years, the gas may condense and grow hot again and form new stars; around some stars there will be worlds; and on some worlds there will be life. The stars will go on rushing apart, until gravity saves them at the last, when they have grown infinitely distant . . . then they will rush together again. When everything has shrunk to a single point, the point can explode into a new beginning.[11]

Against such a backdrop – an epic drama of beginnings and endings, of destructions and rebirths – our own preoccupations assume their appropriate scale. Likewise, on the Malvern hills in the summer of 2002, while I stood on top of the Worcestershire Beacon reflecting uncertainly on the longer-term prospects of unemployment and insecurity, it was impossible not to be distracted and drawn in by the glory of the natural landscape as, day after day, piece by piece, it revealed its treasures. There in the west, out beyond the fruit groves and orchards of Herefordshire, and still further out past the Black Mountains of Powys, as the sun sank once more behind the stolid bulk of British Camp, and my face was brushed by the gentle breeze of evening, I could sense a real enchantment in the air – but an enchantment which, like that in John Cowper Powys' fictional Glastonbury, perhaps could not fully be detected 'anywhere in this rain-drenched town . . . not in all this Gwlad-yr-Haw of Somerset . . . perhaps not anywhere in all the round earth!'[12] The landscape seemed to reach beyond itself for a mystery which defied articulation, which suggested cosmic truths inaccessible to human thought or speech, but which nevertheless comforted and reassured by virtue of its sheer antiquarian bulk and grandeur. For this was indeed a very ancient topography. The Malvern hills were formed six hundred million years ago, in the pre-Cambrian era, at a time when the land they now occupy was somewhere south of the equator and was part of a supercontinent called Pangaea by geologists. Their weathered humps proclaim participation in a story whose epic and eventful longevity, over countless winters and summers, we can barely conceive. Measured against such a mellow, desiccated dignity, the thrusting peaks of the world's higher mountains must be counted callow and youthful newcomers.[13] The impression left by such a landscape is that of what Robert Macfarlane (echoing John McPhee), in his splendid cultural history of mountains, *Mountains of the Mind*, calls 'deep time': an awesome process of ageing and maturation that almost surpasses the capacity of human beings to measure it, such is the grand time frame according to which it operates. As Macfarlane says,

Contemplating the immensities of deep time, you face, in a
way that is both exquisite and horrifying, the total collapse of
your present, compacted to nothingness by the pressures of
pasts and futures too extensive to envisage. And it is a
physical as well as a cerebral horror, for to acknowledge that
the hard rock of a mountain is vulnerable to the attrition of
time is of necessity to reflect on the appalling transience of the
human body.[14]

Yet despite the fact that such a daunting timescale threatens
almost to overwhelm our sense of self, it does not crush the
human spirit. For as Macfarlane adds, 'there is also something
curiously exhilarating about the contemplation of deep time.
True, you learn yourself to be a blip in the larger projects of the
universe. But you are also rewarded with the realization that you
do exist – as unlikely as it may seem, you do exist.'[15]

To reflect appropriately on the essentially surprising nature of
our existence, and to do so against the stunning backdrop of a
landscape such as that viewed from the summits of the Malvern
hills, is to be awed into humility that participation of our individual consciousnesses in such an experience has been made
permissible at all. And acknowledgement of that insight leads
one to be thankful for the life and privileges one has, whatever
the personal misfortunes and injustices (which are relativised by
those of others, especially in the developing countries) that one
also has to bear. Reflection on the powers at work in the natural
world, and on the time scale by which they – quite literally –
move mountains, leads one to a different sort of contemplation:
a meditative appreciation of existence where human beings are
not so central, not so separate, but are just one part of a whole
cycle of cosmic movements, whether of glaciers, moraine or
mountain peaks, or of combusting suns, new planets and shooting stars. We are all part of the tapestry that interconnects the
universe, and that tapestry is greater than the sum of its parts.
But the beauty of the tapestry depends, of course, on the work-
manship of each thread, and the singularity and craft of each
individual scene depicted on the cloth. That is why we need to
focus on the big picture, and to consider that if we are over-
indulged at the expense of our fellows – if social justice is not at

the forefront of our concerns and preoccupations, whether they be political, or cultural, or religious – then we are letting ourselves down badly, and failing to live up to our full capacity as socially oriented and divinely endowed human beings. In concentrating compassionately and humanely on our corner of the weave, which means considering the consequences of prioritising ourselves over others, and adjusting that behaviour accordingly, we are progressively made aware of how we are contributing to a larger and more inspiring canvas. Ursula Le Guin writes of such an attitude as this as one that has to be learned anew, in contradistinction to that very world of nature from which human beings should be taking their inspiration:

> An act is not . . . like a rock that one picks up and throws, and it hits or misses, and that's the end of it. When that rock is lifted the earth is lighter, the hand that bears it heavier. When it is thrown the circuits of the stars respond, and where it strikes or falls the universe is changed. On every fact the balance of the whole depends . . . But we, insofar as we have power over the world and over one another, we must *learn* to do what the leaf and the whale and the wind do of their own nature. We must learn to keep the balance. Having intelligence, we must not act in ignorance. Having choice, we must not act without responsibility.[16]

In a context where imaginative reflection on the character of time and landscape have a real pedagogical value, it is possible that one's perceptions of the world and its meanings can be transformed. We have seen in previous chapters how *remembering* the world enables us meaningfully to hold together past, present and future, and this is true also in its application to deep time, where from generation to generation recollection has been used to articulate the myths, seasonal rhythms and topographic alterations of the ever-changing landscape. For example, for centuries the notion endured in folksongs and bardic lays that our ancestors used to hunt in great forests now lost beneath the sea (a notion given renewed vitality by the related strands of the Atlantis legend). Recent seismic discoveries of Palaeolithic human settlements abandoned beneath the North Sea and

English Channel, when meltwater flooded the land bridges link-
ing Britain to the continent at the end of the last ice age, indicate
that such communities of hunters – as well as the forests and
great river valleys in which they used to hunt – existed in fact,
and not just in legend.[17] Buried in the substratum of human
memory is the key to unlocking the secrets of how we once lived.
But the secrets do not necessarily rise easily to the surface, and
people now have to struggle, just as their ancestors did, to make
sense of their lives in their own specific locales and in debate
with their own unique concerns. What we can do, with the
proto-memories that we have had handed down from our prede-
cessors, is reconnect with a landscape they too inhabited, and
adopt towards it, just as they did, an appropriate sense of reverence and awe within which we may detect the true ground of our
being. This means letting go of the notion that we exist at the
centre of the world and putting creation and its Creator back to
where they belong in our personal hierarchies – right at the
centre, not out at the periphery where they may quietly be
forgotten or exploited. Perhaps the greatest challenge posed to
all religion today is how adequately and intelligently to articulate the mystery of God. The Christian churches in the West have
struggled mostly unsuccessfully with this conundrum. New Age
manifestations do so with varying degrees of credibility, attrac-
tiveness and success. But as I have suggested in this book, so
often it seems to be within nominally secular accounts, which
rely for their power on storytelling and creative myth-making,
that the contemporary hunger for 'meaning' is most richly
satisfied. In an age of fragmentedness and confusion, where
terrorism and climate change are evoked as the twin catastro-
phes of our time, we need to 'come of age' by abandoning tired
narratives which no longer speak to our necessities, and look
instead to our own best resources for meaning. The most
effective of these have an authenticity which resonates with our
deepest needs as human beings, because within them we recognise the atavistic truth of shared experience, as well as the
visionary power to change things for the better.[18]

The notion of 'deep time' (in conjunction with the imaginative
reflection that I was able to conduct on my many treks over the
Malvern hills) helped me to see that the loss of my job in 2002 –

while certainly disagreeable and frightening – was not, and should never have been viewed as, the whole picture. True fulfilment may come over a period of many years, and should not be sought necessarily just in one location or within the confinement of a short period of 'satisfactions'. In one of the most powerful passages in his book, Robert Macfarlane shows that something that has taken a great deal of time to evolve – like a brilliantly complex and subtle wine – may show off its glories all the more potently when finally its innermost character is fully revealed:

> Once, halfway up the mica-ridge peak of Ben Lawers in Scotland on a sunlit day, I found a square chest of sedimentary rock, hinged at its back with an overgrowth of moss and grass. Stepping back and looking at it from the side, I could see it was composed of hundreds of thin layers of grey rock, each one no thicker than a sheet. Each layer, I reckoned, was a paraphrase of 10,000 years – a hundred centuries abbreviated into three millimetres' depth of rock.
>
> Between the grey layers I noticed a thin silvery stratum. I pushed the adze of my walking axe into the rock, and tried to lever the strata apart. The block cracked open, and I managed to get my fingers behind the heavy top lid of rock. I lifted, and the rock opened. And there, between two layers of grey rock, was a square yard of silver mica, seething brightly in the sunlight – probably the first sunlight to strike it in millions of years. It was like opening a chest filled to the brim with silver, like opening a book to find a mirror leafed inside it, or like opening a trapdoor to reveal a vault of time so dizzyingly deep that I might have fallen head-first into it.[19]

In just such a way should one look to fulfilment to come slowly and not necessarily always to be visible at once. Our world, like the Malvern hills which are part of it, has evolved very gradually, and the myriad diversity and complexity that are so integral to its wonder have taken eons to mature and come to fruition. An appropriate sense of temporal hiddenness should help us to put our own lives in perspective. Nicholas Wolterstorff is I think correct when he reflects that '"A religion which does not affirm that God is hidden is not true. *Vere tu es deus absconditus* – truly you are a hidden God" (Pascal). Perhaps it has been a mistake to think that God reveals himself. He speaks, yes. But as he speaks, he hides. His face he does not show us.'[20]

As I have already remarked, God can often seem far away and undetectable to prayer or contemplation. But perhaps it is as much in his absence as his presence that he shows to us his real face. In affliction and the endurance of adversity God is with us, just as he is present in joy and hope, and within such endurance sometimes he is able to show us that our immediate proccupations are not what they seem or do not deserve the pessimism we attach to them. By this reckoning, and keeping in mind the hidden and gradualist nature of true fulfilment, certainly work alone – the manna of so many contemporary British workers – should not by itself provide the summation of meaning and purpose. Madeleine Bunting has correctly and comprehensively shown (in her recent book *Willing Slaves*) that 'the overwork culture is one of the main contributors to a crisis in human sustainability, because it is depriving us of the time and energy to sustain and nurture lives.'[21] The workplace increasingly has taken on the role of a sort of surrogate church, where religious as much as secular value is sought in sitting unproductively at one's desk from morning till night, and where – in a sort of warped apotheosis of the Protestant work ethic – personal industriousness has come to be equated with fundamental worth. As Bunting says,

> The corporation speaks the language of a religious institution – 'meaning' – and, confusingly, the language of love. 'Passion' has slipped from bedroom to boardroom, and spread like a contagion throughout management-speak; the word carries connotations of both emotional intimacy and strength of purpose. The language used to articulate brand values is elastically stretched to accommodate contradictions and confusions in evocative phrases intended to obfuscate – to window-dress – the sometimes brutal workings of the organisation, as well as to inspire. Employees are subjected to mission statements, vision statements, brand values, all of which are designed to capture their hearts, minds and souls.

Employees, in a deceptively egalitarian spirit (not borne out by
the pay structure) are known as 'colleagues' in Asda, or
'partners' in Starbucks; 'human resources' – itself a
comparatively recent replacement for the earlier 'personnel
department' – has taken on pleasantly democratic overtones as
the 'people department'; and companies are very fond indeed
of instituting 'communities' in place of departments, while
'positions', not people, are made redundant.[22]

Alternative religiosities may well represent much of value, but
overweening banality of this sort is surely taking a road to
nowhere. In our new century, the culture of overwork is a blight
on British social and cultural life, and the insecurity and the fear
which underlie it (superbly documented by Bunting in a book
that will surely come to be seen as the definitive account of how
office workers in the UK have allowed themselves, over the last
decade, to be hoodwinked into working so unprofitably and
unproductively) are now manifested in the language and
conceptuality of *faux*-spirituality. The 'Wal-Mart chant' has
replaced formalised worship. Team hugs are cashing in on the
sincere desire of most human beings for contact and intimacy.
This is sacrilege: people are assigned value only to the extent
that they clear the emails in their inbox by the end of the day.
The unexpected fillip of having a breathing space, or interreg-
num, from the culture of work, was that for the first time
since university I was able to recognise, in an important and
personal sense (when I was able to reconnect with the energies
of a world 'out there'), that there was much more to life than
work, and that life's meaning has to be found in an appropriately holistic context where fulfilment is realised not just over
time, but in a plethora of different ways, which impact dutifully
and lovingly upon the world, and not least upon those to whom
one is closest. The proper development and unpacking of a con-
ception of fulfilment such as this might point towards a new
kind of society, where, as Bunting puts it, we could 'effect the
political and personal change to tame technology and the global
economy to meet human needs, rather than exploit human vul-
nerabilities'.[23]

Once again, it is especially within the work of contemporary novelists that so often I find poignant and pertinent notions of fulfilment. The idea of deep time is explored with haunting beauty in a largely forgotten and now difficult to find mountaineering novel by Christopher Burns, called *The Condition of Ice*, first published in 1990. It is remarkable that many of Robert Macfarlane's preoccupations have been prefigured in fiction by Burns' book – which may suggest that anyone with a serious interest in mountains soon comes to reflect on the sorts of metaphysical and existential concerns which thoroughly engage both writers. In Burns' version of the human obsession with mountains, and the desire to climb them, the themes of love, loss and fulfilment are interwoven in so central a way that his account of them seems to endorse my own view that these are among the most fundamental locations for life's 'meaning'. The novel is told from the perspective of an Englishman called Ernest Tinnion, who leaves England in the 1930s to attempt the first ascent of the north face of the Versücherin ('the Temptress') with his childhood friend, Hansi Kirchner, who is Swiss. Tinnion is accompanied by his lover Jean, who has abandoned her husband for Ernest, but who comes to sees in the men's cause and devotion to the mountain merely grand folly and the selfish desire for a glorious death.

Over the glowering bulk of the mountainside and the impending assault on it looms a yet greater threat: that of the outbreak of war, which we know will soon engulf the whole of Europe together with its competing, but at present still friendly, mountaineers. At a later point in the novel, just before the fateful ascent, Ernest takes his lover on a day trip to explore a nearby glacier. Initially Ernest is reluctant to explore the glacier's interior, but at Jean's prompting he finally relents and leads her inside. While reflecting that Ernest's dead body may eventually be returned to her after his unsuccessful ascent of the mountain, by the inexorable movement of the glacier's flow, Jean picks up a pebble from the 'eerily smooth bedrock' of the glacier's base, which she intends to keep as a memento of their trip, and then predicts of Ernest:

> You'll vanish from my sight, and I'll think you have run away.
> But years later, an old woman, I'll be brought to see your body

lying at the bottom of a glacier. You'll be just as you are now – hair, fingernails, even the little cut you made while shaving this morning. They'll know who you are by the papers in your pockets, but I'll have to come along to identify the lover of my youth.[24]

But in an ironic twist we learn that it is the fate of Jean, not Ernest, to be killed, and that it is her remains, not his, which must later be identified. After Ernest has indeed succeeded in climbing the Versücherin (during this achievement his partner Hansi has frozen to death, and Ernest is compelled to cut his corpse loose from the climbing rope which, in death and in life, had bound the two friends together), Jean – disillusioned by Tinnion's selfishness – abandons him for a German photo-grapher with sinister and fanatical Nazi predilections, called Max Volkwein. At the very end of the novel (when Max and Ernest have met again as old men at a formal reunion organised to celebrate the conquest of the Versücherin), we are told that Jean's severed arm, 'complete from elbow to finger', was recov-ered by Max after an Allied bombing raid: and that this was the only remnant of her to be preserved. In a moment where the past overtakes the present, and Tinnion's memories of his relation-ship with Jean prove almost overpowering, Max hands him the pebble which Jean had retained from her visit with Ernest to the glacier: '"Jean used to play with that all the time," Max said. "She passed it from hand to hand like a favourite toy. She must have left it somewhere – as you can see, it is still smooth, and the blast has hardly touched it. We found it weeks later among the rubble. Does it mean anything to you?"'[25]

It seems that despite Jean's apparent betrayal of him (which was itself prompted by his betrayal of a life with her for the sake of securing a questionable glory on the mountain), Ernest – whose memory she evoked by the pebble she kept – remained lodged in Jean's thoughts to the end. The implication is that perhaps, even when living in Germany, his country's enemy, she continued to love him, until her life ended abruptly in the charred and smouldering rubble of an air-raid. Ernest pays tribute to his own memory of Jean in such a way that the irre-pressible capacity of the human spirit to love and to cope with loss is appropriately commemorated on the very summit of the Versücherin. While an official ceremony to honour the mountain's conquerors is taking place there, Tinnion seizes the moment to conduct a private ceremony of his own:

> The summit shone with light, and the air was so pure that it caught in my throat. All around me was the whirr of camera motordrives. I walked through the sunlight and the icy air towards the cairn.
>
> The stones had been unpacked from one side of the cairn, leaving a recess. The new logbook had been placed near by on top of a folding pedestal. It was open at the first page so that we, the survivors, could all sign it. I was the first name. There was a scattering of applause when I signed it, and stepped away.
>
> As the others queued up for their turn, I edged my way back to the cairn. When I was sure that no one was looking, I took the pebble from my pocket and placed it within the recess. There was a gap between two of the stones at the bottom of the hollow; I pushed the pebble between them and it vanished. I heard it click as it tumbled and slid within the cairn, then rested at its heart. It would never be found.
>
> Around us, for mile upon mile, the mountains were ranged in an infinity of ridges, and fell into numberless valleys. It was the first time I had seen the view from the top of the Versücherin.[26]

The climax of Christopher Burns' novel forms a fitting note with which to conclude this chapter. For in Burns' book we find encapsulated the idea, expressed movingly and with great economy of expression, that fulfilment may arrive in unexpected ways, and that such fulfilment may sometimes also be the culmination of love and loss. In the movement of mountains, in the melting of glaciers, and in the burial of secrets within the heart of the earth, may be detected the mysteries of a universe which expresses itself unpredictably, over time, and in the sudden gleam of long-lost mica exposed to virgin sunlight. What is exposed and what is hidden may later on be hidden and exposed in their turn, as the processes of deep time lay bare or conceal what presently our eyes may and may not see. In contemplating the cosmic drama of creation, whether of the death of stars, or the erosion of mountaintops, or the volcanic emergence of new islands, we see again and again – as we have seen throughout this book – that loss can be gain, just as gain may be loss. If they are to be found anywhere, the meanings of life lie in an appropriate and considered reflection on the multifaceted and often contradictory nature of fulfilment as this is mediated to us over the entire course of our lives. And not just in our lives, but in the life, too, of the whole planet and the sentient cosmos to which we are indubitably bound as if by gossamer threads.

CONCLUSION

Meanings of Life

In my last book my concern was to explore aspects of what might be called 'secular theology' in order to make greater sense of the Christian tradition within a context of fragmentation, all-pervasive change, and disconnectedness from previously established assumptions and givens. My aim was to try to establish the grounds for a series of constructive conversations, first of all between the Church and its theologians, and second between Church and world, so that instead of dissonance and deafness between essentially ghettoised constituencies there should rather be renewed understanding and a sense of mutual recognition: Western society and the Church would – as a result of an appreciation of each other's many richnesses and creative resources – gain an enhanced idea of how each could learn from and benefit the other. In this new book, I have tried to take further my previous interest in exploring and encouraging creative interchange. This has turned out not to be a decisive or tightly compartmentalised book, but has emerged – in keeping with the postmodern outlook by which my thinking has been influenced – impressionistically and unsystematically, as a variety of categories and topics have come into frame one by one, like hikers looming out of the mist, only to disassemble like footprints washed away by the tide. I have not set out to offer firm solutions, but have wanted rather to discuss issues open-mindedly and non-prescriptively, and to connect with a variety of metaphysical material like water running over stone – that is, with a hoped-for naturalness and sense of empathy.

While avoiding, for reasons already mentioned, discussions of what constitutes 'spirituality', or of specific 'spiritualities', I have nonetheless attempted to offer a book that is decidedly spiritual, in that I have tried to examine here some of the many roots and springs by which human beings nourish their inner lives. The Christian tradition, though it breaks through the ether from time to time, has been rather less prominent than I would have predicted when I wrote the previous book. My experiences within various religious institutions must be held at least partly responsible for its abscondment. But my chief motivation for wanting to write about meaning from a variety of perspectives, secular as well as religious, has been the desire to 'connect' with the very many people who, like me, do not see in Christianity the answers to the questions they are asking. The deepest questions of human existence remain as popular and pertinent as ever, but increasingly they seem resistant to Christian incursion.

My reflections on 'meanings of life' have taken the form of a cycle of meditations on my own memories and on what I have called 'remembrances': a number of defining moments in, or aspects of, my life within which I believe some locus of enduring or transcendent significance may be discerned. My hope is that others will recognise in those 'moments of meaning', and in the reflections that have followed them, some corresponding resonance and sense of connectedness to similarly definitive or memorable turning points in their own lives. Love, loss and fulfilment have all been touched on, and the book has attempted, in its perhaps idiosyncratically meditative and reflective format, to say something meaningful about (and even representative of) a few of the keenest preoccupations of the contemporary Western mind – whether about its fears and its dreads, or its aspirations and its dreams. In engaging with the 'big issues', my aim has been to point – very tentatively and haltingly – to some of the tensions that may exist between individualism and community, and to how people might consider reconciling their own needs with the wider demands of the communities which shape them, as well as the macro imperatives of the planet itself. This has meant reflecting on the essential interrelatedness of

creation and its Creator, as well as on the beneficent and transcendent presence which I believe suffuses our world and what
lies beyond it. A defining characteristic of the book has been
its emphasis on the profundity and sanctity of all life – held
together by an encompassing *ur*-Spirit or Energy to which
human identity is integrally connected and indissolubly bound.
Various notions of the transcendent, as these intersect with the
life of human beings and their preoccupations, have been
explored, especially through the heuristic of storytelling –
notably in secular accounts mediated through drama, fiction and
film.

As I see it, the stories we tell, especially, though not exclusively, as these are articulated through recollection and remembrance, enable us to connect with those worlds and people we
have lost, and thus to bind ourselves meaningfully to our pasts,
presents and futures. Through an appropriate meditation on the
diversity of the stories we recount, and on the profundity of
what a notion of time extending beyond our own lives may tell
us about the nature of how those lives are 'completed', we are
brought face to face with the living reality that is the ground and
source of our being. Such meditation highlights the choices that
now confront us in a context of limited planetary resources, religious and ideological conflict, and of unchecked technological
development at the expense of consideration and compassion
for the people who are our neighbours. My focus throughout
has been on trying to relate instances of religious and secular
wisdom to the real situations and spiritual needs of people in
the twenty-first century, with a view to offering them a pragmatic roadmap that they can use, whether for personal growth,
individual meditation, or for group study and discussion.

Where, then, are our meanings of life to be found in this brave
new world of the twenty-first century? I do not believe they
are necessarily to be located in the pronouncements or the
formalised ritual of church-based institutions, whose capacity
to reach out effectively to the people they serve seems to be
increasingly open to question. I believe rather that they are to be
found in a mature, humane consideration for others and their
welfare; in an appropriate cultivation of reverence for all life,
which is manifested in the complex web of interconnected

threads that touches us all; and in appropriate meditation and
reflection upon the living reality of the universe from which we
emerge and to which in the end we return. Such reflection and
meditation means acknowledging the limits which are necessarily set upon language, and on our capacity to conceptualise
reality by rational or scientific enquiry. As John Bowker rightly
reminds us,

> It is essential to learn the lessons of this century in
> understanding more clearly the relations between language
> and reference, symbol and sign, icon and index. In particular,
> we now see more clearly that whilst all our languages, theories
> and pictures are approximate, provisional, corrigible and
> frequently wrong, they may nevertheless be wrong (on many
> occasions of our using them) about something; and that
> 'something' then sets a limit on language by being what it is,
> even though we can never describe exactly or exhaustively
> what it is. This is even true of something so relatively obvious
> as the universe. Truth can therefore be told in fiction as well as
> in fact, by way of poetry as well as by way of proof.[1]

There is value to be had, therefore, in reflecting on the 'hidden'
as much as on the 'revealed' nature of transcendent meaning.
Rowan Williams recognises as much when he talks about the
importance of understanding the dichotomy between 'the
murderously spiritual and the compassionately secular',[2] or of
recognising that religion does not always have better access to
truth than a secular outlook characterised by a genuinely compassionate and empathic concern for others. In fact, religion may
be used as an excuse or justification for acts of violence or terror.
Williams talks about the fact that his memories of 9/11 (in whose
horrific events he was himself bound up) include a recollection
of actions that did not add up to a self-important devotion to
some supposedly noble or higher purpose (like the hijackers of
the planes which wrought such destruction and mayhem), but
were rather quietly fulfilled and non-egotistical expressions of
whole lifetimes of service and duty conducted on behalf of the
whole community:

Memories of that morning for me include the enormously careful calm of one of the building staff, trained as a volunteer fire-officer, deliberately talking us through the practical things to do next; and of the staff who were supervising the children's day care centre on the first floor, putting their own fear on hold while they reassured the children. Small examples of what was visible in much more costly ways outside, a couple of streets away. If we are to remember 11 September 2001, we had better remember this too; for example, that one fire-fighting unit in New York lost all its members that day. It puts a different perspective on heroism for a moment. It tells us that heroism is not always bound up with drama, the sense of a Great Cause, but is something about doing what is necessary for a community's health and security. For most of the time, this will be invisible; it is only in crisis that the habits slowly and even drearily formed over years emerge to make possible what can be seen only as extraordinary and selfless labours.[3]

It is precisely in the ordinary that so often we are brought face to face with the extraordinary. In the countless 'small examples' (as Rowan Williams puts it) of loyalty, generosity, consideration, selfless compassion and love, on the part of individuals, which enable their communities to function from day to day, from year to year, and beyond, we see reflected the true nature of 'meaning' and of what life's real value might be said to consist. That is why I have given such emphasis in this book to the idea of 'secular spirituality': that the transcendent may be discerned as much in novels, film-making and poetry – in the imaginative resources by which we make sense of the world, and which extend back to the *proto*-memories and perceptions of our ancestors – as it may in more readily accepted locales like religious ritual and communal liturgy.

In his novel *Out of the Line of Fire*, Mark Henshaw tells a marvellous parable which in poetical and impressively compressed form encapsulates the idea that 'meaning' may come to us in very unexpected ways. Henshaw shows that what may at first be concealed indicates, when finally brought to the light, that a true understanding of what something 'means' may only be revealed over the fullness of time. Since it provides so apposite a commentary on the themes of this book, the parable is worth reproducing in its entirety:

> Every man, woman and child knew the name Chavez, the man who had been transformed overnight from a despised traitor into a national hero.
> And one day he would teach his own son the story of how this tiny elf of a man had been compelled by the military dictatorship to compose a national anthem for their country and how after the revolution he had been denounced for acts of treason against the people. He would tell him of how eminent scholars, noted musicians and distinguished conductors had all testified against him, claiming his music embodied the 'oppressiveness of the overthrown regime' and the 'regimentation of the human spirit'.
> He would tell him how he had been at his trial, how he had seen Chavez standing there openly, sometimes uncontrollably, laughing at their testimony, but saying nothing. His behaviour had scandalised the court. The presiding judges had had to call repeatedly for order. After all the evidence against him, apparently conclusive, had been heard, Chavez, still beaming, was asked if he had anything to say before sentence was passed. He did. He asked that an orchestra be brought before the court to hear the offending piece. After a long discussion his request was agreed to and the court adjourned.
> The next day an orchestra was assembled in the courtroom and after tuning up, and with Chavez back in the witness stand, it began to play. Immediately tears of laughter began to stream down his face. He slapped his knees with glee, bent double and hooted as the march changed tempo, chortled to himself as through he'd been told the funniest joke of his life when the music modulated into a minor key and then, for the remainder of the piece, stood before the court red-faced and trembling with barely suppressed laughter. Everyone, including the judges, thought his mind had become unhinged.
> Finally the last notes died away. It was some time before Chavez could pull himself together. The three judges sat there outraged.

Is that all you have to say for yourself? one of them finally asked.

No, your Honour, he said. With the court's permission I would like the orchestra to play the piece again.

Again! said the judge.

Yes, your Honour. But this time with one change. I want them to play it backwards from the end. And slowly, very slowly. A murmur passed around the crowded courtroom. Was this a joke? Was this man really mad? The players looked at each other with puzzled expressions of their faces and then at the music.

Absolute silence settled over the courtroom as the musicians took up their instruments again.

Slowly, hauntingly, a single cello began to play. A stark, seven-note melody of ethereal beauty floated up to fill the air above their heads. It rose and rose, and then seemed to hover, to stagger, and then to die away. Then a chorus of violins repeated this motif in a long, lingering answer until finally the whole orchestra was swept away by the music, drowned in an elegiac hymn of such haunting tenderness that each person in the courtroom, from the chief presiding judge to the most humble peasant, felt shamed, shamed to the soul that they had called this man a traitor. It was as though in his music Chavez had incorporated their entire history, their suffering, their defeat, their tragedy and, ultimately, their victory such was its greatness.

When finally the last note had sounded a strange silence had settled back over the courtroom.[4]

A parable of this kind, though it is not overtly 'religious', has the capacity to – as Tina Beattie puts it in another context – 'lead us surreptitiously and unawares into a moving meditation on the meaning of beauty and the purpose of life. There is a point when a bleak but entertaining comedy mutates into something different, as grace creeps in by stealth and we begin to see things differently.'[5] The tale of Chavez, the unfairly vilified and ulti-mately vindicated composer, whose entire being was oriented towards articulating in his music the soul and spirit of his home-land, gives us access to a wider, more transcendent perspective on the world – wherein things we think we know take on a wholly different hue, and are then transformed into the wondrous and life-changing. A similar transformational effect is evident in Sam Mendes' Oscar-winning film *American Beauty* (1999), and in the now famous and much discussed series of shots of a plastic bag buffeted by the breeze. As Beattie perceptively writes of the movie:

> There is a sequence which lingers in the imagination long after the film is over. Ricky shows Jane a blurry video of a plastic bag blowing in the wind among autumn leaves. As they watch he explains that 'this bag was, like, dancing with me. Like a little kid begging me to play with it . . . And that's the day I knew there was this entire life behind things, and this incredibly benevolent force, that wanted me to know there was no reason to be afraid. Ever.' That, Ricky says, is why he uses his video camera. 'It helps me to remember – and I need to remember.' Much later in the film, we see that video clip again and it becomes a quiet affirmation of a life gratefully remembered in the dawn of eternity . . . *American Beauty* shows us a way of remembering and a way of seeing, so that like Lester we come to know beauty as something that 'flows through me like rain and I can't feel anything but gratitude for every single moment of my stupid little life'.[6]

Such a mediation of the unexpected and the hidden – of the sense of beauty or 'meaning' coming to us gradually, over time, and not instantaneously, or in terms solely of self-gratification – may point towards a way in which our lives can be completed and made 'whole'. We need to keep in mind that there is a boundary beyond which none of us can see, a border beyond which we cannot go. Down on the shore, amidst the jetsam and flotsam of the receding tideline, we catch glimpses of lives other than our own which contextualise and lend insight to our personal concerns. We are part of them, and they of us. And beyond the floating detritus of those other lives, we see something more – something Else: the animating spirit of the universe whose manifestations are so complex, sacred and all-encompassing that they should invoke a response of reverence and awe. Our lives come and go, and the footprints we have left on the sand are indeed erased by the implacable current of the waves as they roar unceasingly over the beach. But in the magnificent diversity of creation is the legacy of our individuality: the unity to which we are all bound, which is all One, and precious.

Loss, is gain; gain is loss. At my grandfather's funeral I stood by the lectern and read the following words, which were left as a legacy by a soldier killed in northern Ireland 'to all my loved ones'. In them, as in all the wonder and mystery of the pantheistic world they evoke, we begin, tentatively and fragmentedly, to see where life's true meanings lie:

> Do not stand at my grave and weep,
> I am not there; I do not sleep.
> I am a thousand winds that blow,
> I am the diamond glints on snow,
> I am the sunlight on ripened grain,
> I am the gentle autumn rain.
> When you awaken in the morning's hush
> I am the swift uplifting rush
> Of quiet birds in circled flight.
> I am the soft starlight at night.
> Do not stand at my grave and cry,
> I am not there; I did not die.[7]

Notes

Preface and Acknowledgements

1. In a bad-tempered review in the *Tablet* (27 April 2002) Bernard Green accused the book of 'smugness', 'anger' and hypocrisy, while seemingly unaware of the log in his own eye. Clearly irritated beyond measure by the author's honest attempt to bring theology into dialogue with contemporary secular thought, he wrote: 'It seems odd to complain that the Churches fail to engage with the world around them and just keep drawing on their own canon of teaching and texts that have nourished Christian thought for centuries, when Wright's account of the world is drawn from his own canon of recent texts that interest him.' Meanwhile, writing in the *Methodist Recorder* (6 June 2002), Leslie Griffiths decided to brush the troubling elements of the book's argument aside ('a now-familiar story . . . a grim distortion') and opt instead for psychoanalysis of the author: 'I suspect that this book should be read more as an apologia for Wright's own life than as an accurate or even helpful description of how things lie for organised Christianity. Clearly, in his private life, he's fallen out of love with the whole enterprise. He's not just frustrated with an institution he once loved; he seems bitter, as though it has hurt him or let him down in some personal way.' Griffiths concluded his wholly inaccurate and ignorant personal profile with the patronising words 'God help you Alex! I just hope that writing this book helped its author with his own spiritual needs. And that it will goad others into recognising them.' These critical responses by writers in denominational publications contrasted markedly with appreciative notices in the non-confessional *Sea of Faith* magazine, issue 53 (where in May 2002 David Boulton wrote 'I'd love to see this thought-provoking book in the hands of every theology student in the country') and the academic *Expository Times* (where in vol.

114, no. 8, May 2003, George Newlands praised the book as 'exciting and genuinely thought-provoking' while praising too 'the considerable depth of the writer's spiritual vision'). The reviews appeared to divide, in fact, into those written by people deeply invested in maintaining the status quo, who hated the book, and those (to be fair, not always coming from a non-confessional perspective) by writers prepared to look afresh at the issue of how Church and world interact, and who appreciated what *Why Bother?* was attempting to do.

Introduction: What Does It All Mean?

1. The questions paraphrase the Blade Runner of Ridley Scott's eponymous and influential film of 1982. See *Why Bother with Theology?*, pp. 99–100 for a short discussion of the metaphysics of *Blade Runner.*
2. The recent mainstream success of Alain de Botton's books of popular philosophy, such as *The Consolations of Philosophy* and *Status Anxiety*, is just one indication of such interest.
3. See Julian Young, *The Death of God and the Meaning of Life*, p. 4: 'Camus famously begins *The Myth of Sisyphus* by saying that "There is but one truly serious philosophical problem and that is suicide."' For Young, 'the question of suicide is . . . just a dramatic way of posing the question of life's worth or value' (p. 161). His conclusion is that 'for all the many delights of his writing, and for all the credit due to him for looking utterly fundamental issues squarely in the face, Camus is wrong to say that "life . . . will be lived all the better if it has no meaning." The worthwhile life *requires* meaning' (see p. 172).
4. See *October Ferry to Gabriola*, pp. 132–3.
5. See Jamie Doward's report in the *Observer*, 28 March 2004: 'In his Easter message to the diocese of Canterbury, Williams launches a scathing attack on contemporary attitudes, saying that the behaviour of Tanya, Amber and their co-stars in the ITV drama paints an accurate picture of all that is corrupt and uncaring about twenty-first-century priorities . . . The makers of the programme said they shared the archbishop's view that the series was an accurate portrayal of modern Britain.'
6. See Stephen Bates, *A Church at War*, pp. 19–25 and 148–52, for a thoroughly disturbing portrayal of the conservative evangelical attempt to destabilise Rowan Williams' primateship.
7. For example: the patience even of the dependably sympathetic problem-page columnist Mariella Frostrup is stretched to the limit by the attitude of a teenager whose mother complains that she is worried about her 17-year-old son. The woman writes 'He's applied for a place at college but seems apathetic about taking it. He's thinking of taking a gap year but I'm afraid it will make him more indolent. He shows little interest in the world around him unless it's reality TV shows and celebrity magazines.

I couldn't help overhearing him talking to his two best friends the other day and I was shocked by the banality of their discussion (whether Ibiza was "over"). When those bombs went off in Madrid his only response was relief that it wasn't Barcelona, where he is planning a trip at Easter.' To this Frostrup responds: 'It's hard not to feel a shudder of disbelief at the level of vacuity Western society is fast approaching . . . Your teens and twenties are the time to be angry and radical and idealistic. By the time you get to fortysomething you're just too tired (or is that just me?). Yet these days the burden of ideological debate seems to sit firmly on the older generation. It makes for very boring politics. I'm with the chancellor on this one. It's time the nation's youth were dragged from their virtual reality and forced to take a look at the real thing. The Fabian Society may be sceptical, but I think Gordon Brown's plans for Community Service are laudable. A Fabian report by Ruth Fox argues that rather than impose a system which appears punitive in nature, the government should be promoting a scheme that emphasises opportunities, not just obligations. I'm all for obligations. Teenagers already boast the most extreme sense of entitlement. Why should teenagers be encouraged to think that all good deeds get rewarded? The opportunity to spend a year having your eyes opened to the existence of a bigger world, where problems that far outweigh your own exist, should be reward in itself. I'd have them all in uniform doing drill as well, given half the chance!' See 'Dear Mariella', *Observer* Magazine, 28 March 2004.

8. Paul Heelas and Linda Woodhead, *The Spiritual Revolution: Why Religion is Giving Way to Spirituality*, p. 45: 'The holistic milieu is growing whilst the congregational domain is declining. So *if* the holistic milieu continues to grow at the same (linear) rate as it has done since 1970, and *if* the congregational domain continues to decline at the same (linear) rate as it has done during the same period, a spiritual revolution would take place during the third decade of the third millennium.'

9. The British Sociological Association's Sociology of Religion Study Group annual conference in 2004, which was held at Bristol University from 29 March to 1 April on the theme of 'A Sociology of Spirituality' (and which I attended), exemplified both the extraordinary variety of approaches to the study of spirituality, as well as – paradoxically – the difficulty of reaching anything like a consensus about what such 'sprituality' comprises.

10. See Wright, *Why Bother with Theology?*, pp. 18–34, for an overview of postmodernity and some of its chief characteristics.

11. The *Daily Mail*, under the aegis of its full-bloodedly reactionary editor, Paul Dacre, may stake a convincing claim to be the most voluble champion of Middle England in this regard, and in recent years has consistently fulminated against the erosion of what it regards as the rights, interests and privileges of its core readership and constituencies.

Anyone who is subjected second-hand to its daily tirades on a Chilterns commuter train into London, as I have been over the last couple of years, notices the same themes – asylum, benefits, illegal immigrants – wearisomely cropping up over and over again. See Madeleine Bunting, *Willing Slaves: How the Overwork Culture is Ruling our Lives*, pp. 153–4, 'This *stagflation* of Middle England – running harder to stay in the same place – is one of the factors behind the overwork ethic . . . This powerfully drives a sense of grievance in Middle England that they don't enjoy the "just deserts" of their labour; they compare their own position with increasing wealth at the top end of the labour market, and measure the relative decline. The resentment is evident in the aggressive paranoia seen in the *Daily Mail* and targeted at anyone who can be claimed to be enjoying "unjust deserts", be they asylum seekers, welfare scroungers or lone parents.'

12. See Michael Northcott, *An Angel Directs the Storm: Apocalyptic Religion and American Empire*, pp. 30–5, for a good summary of the geopolitical issues at stake.
13. Madeleine Bunting, 'Reasons to be cheerless', *Guardian*, 1 March 2004.
14. ibid.
15. In *Why Bother with Theology?*, pp. 3–16.
16. Stephen Bates, *A Church at War: Anglicans and Homosexuality*, *passim*. Bates convincingly shows that the brouhaha about homosexuality in the Anglican Communion is as much about power politics and a Militant-esque takeover as it is about the authority and interpretation of particular biblical texts.
17. Will Hutton, 'Heed not the fanatics', *Observer*, 11 April 2004.
18. ibid.
19. ibid.
20. ibid.
21. Gordon Lynch, *After Religion: 'Generation X' and the Search for Meaning*, p. 118.
22. ibid. p. 118.
23. See for example Heelas and Woodhead, *The Spiritual Revolution*; Lynch, *After Religion*; and Paul Heelas, *The New Age Movement: Religion, Culture and Society in the Age of Postmodernity*. However, my earlier book may prove useful for a very cursory overview of alternative spiritualities (*Why Bother with Theology?*, pp. 35–52).
24. In her book *Speaking in Parables: A Study in Metaphor and Theology*, see especially pp. 138–9: 'We all love a good story because of the basic narrative quality of human experience; in a sense, any story is about ourselves, and a good story is good precisely because somehow it rings true to human life.' See also *Metaphorical Theology: Models of God in Religious Language*, p. 2, by the same author: 'The mystics . . . have not restricted their language about God to biblical and traditional imagery, for the

experience of God, the certainty and the immediacy of it, has been the basis for new and powerful religious language.'

25. See Young, *The Death of God and the Meaning of Life*, p. 10, for a useful summary of Plato's distinction between form and reality: 'The things of this world are always *imperfect* copies, *inferior* versions of their originals in the world of true Being . . . In the *Republic*, Plato uses the image of the shadow to express the inferiority of everyday things to their originals. We physical creatures are like prisoners in a cave, chained so that we can only see the rock wall in front of us. Beyond the mouth of the cave behind us are real things which, because they are illuminated by the sun, cast shadows on the wall, shadows which most of us, because we cannot turn around, mistake for the real things themselves.'

26. Jenny Diski, *Stranger on a Train*, p. 146.

27. ibid. pp. 146–7.

Chapter 1: Self and World

1. William Paley (1743–1805), Anglican clergyman and natural philosopher, argued in his book *Natural Theology – Or Evidences of the Existence and Attributes of the Deity Collected from the Appearances of Nature* (1802) that the very complexity and design of the natural world evidenced its creator, and in so doing introduced the famous image of the divine watchmaker. In his book *The Blind Watchmaker* (1986), contemporary zoologist and philosopher of science Richard Dawkins argued that Darwin's theory of natural selection made a nonsense of Paley's idea, since natural selection has no grand purpose or design in mind: 'It has no mind and no mind's eye. It does not plan for the future. It has no vision, no foresight, no sight at all. If it can be said to play the role of watchmaker in nature, it is the *blind* watchmaker' (see p. 5). Much of the contemporary debate about the relationship between science and religion, and about the sense they each make of the world, has been characterised by the attempts of theologians and philosophers of religion to respond to Dawkins' rationalistic and deterministic positions, argued in a succession of books, which have been both influential and popular.

2. *The Lord of the Rings*, p. 957: 'Far above the Ephel Dúath in the West the night-sky was still dim and pale. There, peeping among the cloud-rack above a dark tor high up in the mountains, Sam saw a white star twinkle for a while. The beauty of it smote his heart, as he looked up out of the forsaken land, and hope returned to him. For like a shaft, clear and cold, the thought pierced him that in the end the Shadow was only a small and passing thing: there was light and high beauty for ever beyond its reach.'

3. A discussion of how the problem of evil might be related to the idea of God (theodicy) lies outside the purview of this book. However, see John

Hick's *Evil and the God of Love* for a classic statement of the central
problems and proposed solutions. See also Beverley Clack and Brian R.
Clack, *Philosophy of Religion: A Critical Introduction*, pp. 49–67.

4. Ursula K. Le Guin, *The Dispossessed: An Ambiguous Utopia*, p. 57.

5. Charles Davis, *Soft Bodies in a Hard World: Spirituality for the Vulnerable*.
Charles Davis, whom I got to know while living and working in
Cambridge in the early 1990s, and who generously gave me a copy of his
book, always struck me as an interesting and compassionate theologian
with strong inclusivist tendencies. See for example his essay 'Beyond
religion' in the volume mentioned above, where on p. 97 he writes:
'Throughout the world a new self-consciousness is struggling to be born
– a global, critical, corporate self-consciousness, in which human beings
of all races, nations and cultures come together in communication and
partnership, acknowledging the unity that binds them together, despite
the persistent plurality of their traditions . . . Christians have to draw out
and make explicit the implicit grounding of the new self-consciousness . . . Christianity will again become a social force if Christians enter
into the freedom of the Spirit, which brings about the genuinely new
and allows us constantly to change, because the Spirit prevents us iden-
tifying God with any particular finite order or his worship with any particular set of religious practices.'

6. Ursula K. Le Guin, *The Dispossessed*, p. 162.

7. For a wonderfully entertaining treatment of some of the most significant
religious views of human identity and the 'meaning' of the world, see
Gore Vidal's novel *Creation*, whose fictional narrator Cyrus Spitama
encounters, during the course of his travels through central, south and
east Asia in the fifth century BCE, the central metaphysical doctrines of,
among others, Zoroaster, the Buddha, Lao Tsu, Confucius, Pythagoras,
and the Jains Gosala and Mahavira.

8. Vernon White, *Identity*, p. 49.

9. ibid.

10. ibid. p. 50.

11. ibid.

12. ibid. p. 49.

13. John Bowker, *The Meanings of Death*.

14. ibid. p. 221.

15. Bowker is always respectful of the value of difference and of perspectives other than his own: for example, when he writes 'We cannot
impose – God forbid – the concept of the fact of sacrifice on others in the
moment of their crisis' (ibid. p. 226).

16. See ibid. p. 227: 'It is a human privilege, just as surely as it is a human
suffering, to acquire consciously the necessary condition of death, and to
affirm it as sacrifice, as the means through which life is enabled and
secured. That, consummately, is what Jesus did on the cross. But it is

what countless others have also done through the long centuries of human history.'

17. ibid. p. 227.

18. ibid. p. 228.

19. ibid.

20. ibid. p. 229.

21. Alan Garner, *Thursbitch*, p. 87.

22. Sebastian Faulks, *Birdsong*, pp. 290–1.

23. See *Why Bother with Theology?*, pp. 81–93.

24. Charles Tomlinson, 'The Santa Fe railroad', from *Annunciations*, p. 7.

25. Barbara Greene and Victor Gollancz (eds), *God of a Hundred Names: Prayers of Many Peoples and Creeds*, p. 242.

26. Brian Bates, *The Real Middle-Earth: Magic and Mystery in the Dark Ages*, p. 87.

27. ibid. p. 46.

28. ibid.

29. ibid. p. 47.

30. ibid.

31. ibid. p. 133.

32. ibid. p. 255. See also Simon Schama's book *Landscape and Memory* for a wonderfully eclectic cultural history of how the landscape has interacted with and impacted on the human imagination. Schama writes on pp. 6–7: 'Although we are accustomed to separate nature and human perception into two realms, they are, in fact, indivisible. Before it can ever be a repose for the senses, landscape is the work of the mind. Its scenery is built up as much from strata of memory as from layers of rock.' Christopher Priest (whose novel *The Affirmation* is discussed in the next chapter) also has a profound appreciation of the linkage between landscape, memory and the imagination. In his novel *A Dream of Wessex* (1977), participants in a scientific experiment called the Ridpath Projection, which is based in a fictional laboratory beneath Maiden Castle, project their mental energies into an imagined future Dorchester in order to try to solve some of the social and economic problems of their own present. As Priest would have it, his brilliantly portrayed world of the twenty-second century, with its notions of a different topography formed by seismic disturbances and earthquakes, a geographically distinct Wessex Island, a new Somerset Sea, and a surging tidal bore and wave riders, is in essence a gestalt brought into being by the collective memories of the Ridpath participants.

33. In their book *The Green Man in Britain*, Fran and Geoff Doel quote Susan Clifford, who highlights the integral relationship of the green man and the goddess: 'The Green Man is taking a part which is a protective part for . . . the female forest or the Earth Mother' (see p. 22). The association is celebrated by a bookshop on Glastonbury's high street called 'The

Goddess and the Green Man' (see www.goddessandgreenman.co.uk), which stocks books and other items relating to both goddess mythology and the green man's origins and significance. Glastonbury has long been a centre of goddess worship. Some think that the spiral maze which winds its way round the Tor may have been dedicated to a goddess whose fertility was also celebrated in the red water of the Chalice Well. And when Christianity came to Britain, Glastonbury's Celtic sanctuary became the country's first centre of the Marian cult. As for the green man, the Doels' book offers fascinating insights into his history and into the Celtic association of the colour green with fertility, enchantment and magic. As the authors drolly point out, it was Christianity which gave green the negative connotations which it laboured under for centuries: 'Medieval Christianity, despite the enlightened efforts of St Francis of Assisi, had a problem with the natural world and the forces of nature. Unlike the Celts, the Christians emphasised the supremacy of man over the rest of God's creation. And the emphasis on the importance of virginity and chastity in Christian theology, which probably derives mainly from its Eastern roots, always sat uneasily in relation to Western societies' (see p. 27).

34. See William Anderson, *Holy Places of the British Isles: A Guide to the Legendary and Sacred Sites*, p. 82: 'There is a spirit about this place, conveyed by the fine air, the views of the intense blue colours of the Somerset countryside, the sense of being taken up above the world, that is most special. Perhaps it is connected with the dedication of the church, whose tower only remains, to the Archangel Michael, the vanquisher of evil, and perhaps every visitor here in climbing the Tor has climbed some way up the mystical hill of the soul and found some release, some sense of a peace that is above the turmoil of passing time.' See also John Michell, *Sacred England: Traveller's Guide to the Legends, Lore and Landscape of England's Sacred Places*, pp. 136–7: 'Over the centuries many stories have been told of people who have found the entrance and gained access to the Tor's inner chambers, where the ancient mysteries were once celebrated. A former abbot of Glastonbury, St Collen in the seventh century, is said to have retired to a hermit's cell at the foot of the Tor, where his contemplations were several times disturbed by that of a strange visitor who demanded that he ascend the hill and pass through a tunnel within it to meet the king of the underworld. Finally he agreed. Armed with a flask of holy water, the saint followed his guide into the bowels of the Tor and confronted Gwynn ap Nudd, the Celtic Lord of Hades, in the midst of his demonic court. A few words were exchanged, then St Collen produced the holy water and dashed it over the king and his demons, who promptly vanished – whereupon the saint found himself alone in the hillside . . . The inside of the Tor does indeed contain passages and chambers, formed by the underground waters which well

up beneath it. Sacred springs once issued from its flanks, and today it conceals a reservoir that supplies the district with water.'

35. Though in Fuqua's impressively gritty version, which differs markedly from John Boorman's earlier, chivalric *Excalibur* (1981), Arthur is portrayed with a reasonable degree of historical verisimilitude as being – as Allan Massie describes him – 'a grim, unromantic figure, fighting a harsh war in the dark period of our history after the withdrawal of the Roman legions'. Massie accepts the thesis recently put forward by Alistair Moffat that Arthur was 'a prince of the Gododdin – the Romanised inhabitants of south-east Scotland who spoke the variant of Celtic known as "P-Celtic" – and that his base was in the Scottish borders.' See 'Arthur', *Independent*, 31 July 2004.

36. Which is recorded as having taken place in the year 537 by the tenth-century *Annals of Wales*, and is described as 'the battle in which the famous Arthur king of the British and Mordred his betrayer fell by wounds inflicted by each other . . .' (see Massie, ibid.).

37. Frederick Bligh Bond (1864–1945) was a colourful individual who deserves reappraisal. A Bristol architect who was put in charge of the Glastonbury Abbey excavations in 1904, he was influenced in his work by spiritualism and automatic writing, and claimed to have discovered the 'sacred geometry' of the Glastonbury site through information provided by the medieval monks of the abbey – the 'Watchers' – whose spokesman was a monk called Johannes Bryant. Unsurprisingly, Bond had a bitter falling out with the then Dean of Wells, Joseph Robinson, and was later sacked in 1922. The *vesica piscis* (Latin for 'fish's bladder') has been used as the basis for many sacred geometric figures, both in antiquity and subsequently, and the cover of the Chalice spring reflects the sacred geometry that Bond detected in the design of the abbey. The symbol also has associations with the moon and the goddess (pagan) and the Virgin and wound in the Christ's side (Christian).

38. According to Michell, the alignment of hill churches later dedicated to St Michael (of which Glastonbury Tor is the grandest of several which also include the famous 'Mump' at Burrowbridge, near Taunton), was in ancient times a pagan pilgrimage route from its westernmost extremity in Land's End to a great temple at Avebury. The sacred power of the landscape was thus recognised in both pagan as well as Christian celebration (see Michell, *Sacred England*, p. 138).

39. See *Sacred England*, p. 141: 'Working from maps and aerial photographs (that) she commissioned, she identified a circle of astrological effigies and other figures which seemed to be referred to in local folklore and place names. Their outlines were marked by streams, tracks, contour lines, and boundaries, and their relative positions were in accordance with a map of the constellations . . . Kathryn Maltwood's idea was that the zodiacal figures were roughly sketched by nature and had been

given more precise form thousands of years ago by the ancient Sumer people of Somerset. No proof is attached to her thesis, but its poetic, visionary quality appeals to many, and it provides a useful synthesis of the various mythological themes which have settled upon the Glastonbury landscape.'

40. Gordon Lynch, *After Religion: 'Generation X' and the Search for Meaning*, p. 115.

41. As Sarah Murgatroyd writes in her book *The Dig Tree: The Extraordinary Story of the Ill-Fated Burke and Wills 1860 Expedition*: 'For Aboriginal people life is inextricably bound to the land, its features, rhythms, animals and its spirits. Every man is the owner and custodian of his own territory, a birthright passed down to him through the male line. A person's identity is forged by their land. The two are inseparable and removal from that place means spiritual as well as physical destruction' (see p. 149).

42. Robyn Davidson, *Tracks*, p. 167.

43. ibid.

44. ibid. p. 108.

45. See *Why Bother with Theology?*, p. 46.

46. Ursula K. Le Guin, *The Farthest Shore*, p. 175.

47. ibid.

Chapter 2: Loss

1. Christopher Priest, *The Affirmation*, p. 61: 'Genuine immortality, medically guaranteed. The clinic claimed a success rate of 100%; no one who ever received the treatment had yet died.'

2. ibid. pp. 63–4.

3. See Barbara J. Bucknell, *Ursula K. Le Guin*, *passim*, for a stimulating discussion of the ways in which Le Guin's work has been influenced by Taoism.

4. Ursula K. Le Guin, *The Farthest Shore*, p. 175.

5. ibid.

6. ibid.

7. ibid. pp. 188–9.

8. Ursula K. Le Guin, *The Dispossessed*, pp. 276–7.

9. John Bowker, *The Meanings of Death*, p. 221.

10. See J. R. R. Tolkien, *The Lord of the Rings*, p. 1067.

11. See *Why Bother with Theology?*, p. 75: 'We recognise again the essential anguish of seeing beautiful and frail things . . . passing away as we read of the Lady Galadriel and the elves making the inevitable journey to the West.'

12. Alison Webster's book *Found Wanting: Women, Christianity and Sexuality*, *passim*, offers a sobering account of how intolerant the church so often

has been of diversity and difference, even when those who call the shots describe themselves as 'liberals'. Individuals who for whatever reason are seen to be an irritant are squashed, obstructed or expelled by those – invariably men – who exercise institutional power. Interestingly, many of those mistreated in this way, who leave the church disillusioned, end up having remarkably successful careers in secular life. See also M. Scott Peck, *People of the Lie*, p. 84, for how self-deception sometimes plays a major part in the psychologies of those who think of themselves as 'religious': 'They cannot or will not tolerate the pain of self-reproach. The decorum with which they lead their lives is maintained as a mirror in which they can see themselves reflected righteously.'

13. Martin Jacques, 'A season in paradise', *Guardian Weekend* magazine, 30 November 2002.
14. ibid.
15. ibid.
16. ibid.
17. ibid.
18. Job 23:17.
19. Stephen Mitchell, *A Book of Psalms: Selected and Adapted from the Hebrew*, p. 26.
20. Job 23:3.
21. Mitchell, *A Book of Psalms*, p. 6.
22. Nicholas Wolterstorff, *Lament for a Son*, pp. 46–7.
23. Bowker, *The Meanings of Death*, p. 227.
24. Wolterstorff, *Lament for a Son*, p. 69.
25. See *Why Bother with Theology?*, pp 65, 110, 120.
26. Le Guin, *The Dispossessed*, p. 57. See also p. 18.
27. Alexander Blok, 'All on the Earth' (1909). This was a poem that meant a lot to me at university, and I made a written note of it at the time. Unfortunately, I do not now possess the translation or publication details. Should any readers be able to provide the missing reference, the publishers and I would be happy to list it in any future printings or editions of this book.
28. *Perfect Strangers* was first broadcast on BBC2 in May 2001. Daniel was played (pre-*Spooks* fame) by Matthew Macfadyen; Rebecca by Claire Skinner; Charles by Toby Stephens; Raymond by Michael Gambon; Esther by Jill Baker; Alice by Lindsay Duncan; and Stephen by Anton Lesser.
29. Stephen Poliakoff, *Perfect Strangers*, p. 211.
30. See my discussion of Hilary Mantel's novel *A Change of Climate* for an interesting parallel: *Why Bother with Theology?*, p. 92.
31. Poliakoff, *Perfect Strangers*, p. 191.
32. ibid.
33. ibid. p. 64.

34. ibid. p. 206.
35. Le Guin, *The Dispossessed*, p. 277.
36. Peter Benson, *The Levels*, p. 134.
37. ibid. p. 137.

Chapter 3: Love

1. Ziyad Marar, *The Happiness Paradox*, p. 98.
2. See Michael Northcott, *An Angel Directs the Storm, passim*, for a good – and passionately written – analysis of the relevant geopolitics.
3. Family Policy Studies Centre (FPSC) findings. See 'Britain singled out as lonely nation', BBC News (news.bbc.co.uk), 27 March 2000.
4. See *Why Bother with Theology?*, pp. 26–31.
5. See pp. 5–6.
6. Wright, *Why Bother with Theology?*, pp. 5–17.
7. See p. 24.
8. Sebastian Faulks, *Birdsong*, pp. 178–9.
9. ibid. p. 182.
10. ibid. p. 280.
11. Wright, *Why Bother with Theology?*, p. 111.
12. Stacy Peebles Power, 'The other world of war: Terrence Malick's adaptation of *The Thin Red Line*' in *The Cinema of Terrence Malick*, ed. Hannah Patterson, p. 153.
13. ibid.
14. ibid. p. 154.
15. Robert Silverman, 'Terrence Malick, landscape and "This war at the heart of nature"' in Patterson (ed.), *The Cinema of Terrence Malick*, p. 170.
16. ibid. p. 171.
17. See Marc Fusteneau and Leslie MacAvoy, 'Terrence Malick's Heideggerian cinema: war and the question of being in *The Thin Red Line*' in Patterson (ed.), *The Cinema of Terrence Malick*, pp. 179–85.
18. ibid. p. 177.
19. See Wright, *Why Bother with Theology?*, pp. 81–7.
20. Colin Thubron, *Turning Back the Sun*, pp. 2–3.
21. ibid. p. 1.
22. ibid. p. 4.
23. ibid. p. 3.
24. ibid. p. 4.
25. ibid. p. 13.
26. ibid. p. 4.
27. ibid. p. 157.
28. ibid. p. 3.
29. ibid. p. 28.
30. ibid. p. 30.

31. ibid.
32. ibid. pp. 28–9.
33. ibid. p. 27.
34. ibid.
35. ibid. p. 58.
36. ibid. p. 61.
37. ibid. p. 23.
38. ibid. p. 21.
39. ibid. p. 141.
40. ibid. p. 142.
41. ibid. p. 144.
42. ibid. p. 157.
43. ibid.
44. ibid. p. 158.
45. ibid.
46. ibid. p. 166.
47. ibid. p. 165.
48. ibid. p. 171.
49. ibid. p. 172.
50. ibid.
51. ibid. pp. 172–3.
52. ibid. p. 176.
53. ibid.
54. ibid. p. 178.
55. ibid. p. 180.
56. ibid. p. 181.
57. ibid. p. 4.
58. ibid. p. 5.
59. ibid.
60. ibid. p. 123.
61. ibid. p. 124.
62. ibid. p. 56.
63. ibid. pp. 202–3.

Chapter 4: Fulfilment

1. Rowan Williams, *Writing in the Dust*, p. 56.
2. ibid. p. 57.
3. ibid. pp. 58–9.
4. Barbara Greene and Victor Gollancz (eds), *God of a Hundred Names*, p. 75.
5. Ziyad Marar, *The Happiness Paradox*, p. 12.
6. Ursula K. Le Guin, *The Dispossessed*, p. 276.
7. See Alex Wright, 'An ambiguous Utopia', *Political Theology* 5:2, April

2004, for a fuller discussion of the religious and other themes of *The Dispossessed*.

8. Le Guin, *The Dispossessed*, p. 277.
9. Brian Bates, *The Real Middle-Earth*, p. 87.
10. See Barbara J. Bucknell, *Ursula K. Le Guin*, p. 30: 'Le Guin takes such obvious pleasure in describing an America returned to the wilderness . . . There is a kind of "small is beautiful" pleasure in following Falk across a continent as he encounters settlements set in mile upon mile of forest followed by prairie.'
11. Maggie Gee, *Light Years*, p. 350.
12. John Cowper Powys, *A Glastonbury Romance*, p. 697.
13. A mere two hundred million years ago, the summits of the Himalayas were lying at the bottom of the vanished Tethys Sea – which is why the fossils of sea creatures can now be found embedded in their rocks by climbers.
14. Robert Macfarlane, *Mountains of the Mind: A History of a Fascination*, pp. 43–4.
15. ibid.
16. Le Guin, *The Farthest Shore*, pp. 74–5.
17. See The Megalithic Portal (www.megalithic.co.uk) for the following story, derived from a news item in the *Observer*, 21 September 2003: 'Herds of reindeer and horses migrated across its plains, huge forests covered much of the countryside and men and women made their homes by rivers and lakes. Then came the deluge, and this ancient Arcadia – which stretched across the North Sea, and covered the Channel – was inundated. All signs of human and animal activity were covered by several hundred feet of water. Only the occasional stone tool, bone harpoon and mammoth tusk, trawled from the sea bed by fishing boats, has provided reminders of this lost world's existence. But the drowned lands of the North Sea and Channel may soon be revealed by British scientists using a revolutionary underwater scanning technique that can create sea-bed maps and images as accurate and detailed as those made of dry land. In the process, the idea of Britain as an island kingdom will be challenged by researchers . . . Ten thousand years ago, at the end of the last ice age, with much of the world's water still trapped in giant glaciers and ice caps, sea levels were many feet below their current level. The river Arun, which now enters the Channel at Littlehampton, then ran on for several miles before flowing into a valley that had been carved by a south-flowing river created by the combined waters of the Thames, Rhine and Seine.'
18. See Wright, *Why Bother with Theology?*, pp. 51–2 for a short discussion of how the value of different spiritualities might be assessed.
19. Macfarlane, *Mountains of the Mind*, p. 65.
20. Nicholas Wolterstorff, *Lament for a Son*, p. 75.

21. Madeleine Bunting, *Willing Slaves: How the Overwork Culture is Ruling our Lives*, p. 211.
22. ibid. p. 116.
23. ibid. p. 325.
24. Christopher Burns, *The Condition of Ice*, p. 54.
25. ibid. p. 167.
26. ibid. p. 170.

Conclusion: Meanings of Life

1. John Bowker, *The Meanings of Death*, p. 210.
2. Rowan Williams, *Writing in the Dust*, p. 13.
3. ibid. pp. 45–7.
4. Mark Henshaw, *Out of the Line of Fire*, pp. 122–4.
5. Tina Beattie, 'Beauty back on camera', *Tablet*, 26 February 2000.
6. ibid.
7. 'Do Not Stand at my Grave and Weep' by Mary E. Frye. See the *Times* obituary of Frye, 5 November 2004, for the definitive version of the poem and for confirmation of her authorship: 'The Baltimore housewife Mary E. Frye was acknowledged towards the end of her long life to be the undisputed author of 'Do Not Stand at my Grave and Weep', the well-known bereavement verse which has brought comfort to mourners throughout the world for 70 years. There were many other claimants to its authorship, including attributions to traditional and native American origins.' The poem was famously read on *Bookworm* on Remembrance Sunday 1995 by the father of soldier Stephen Cummins. Stephen Cummins was killed in Ulster in 1989, aged 24, and left the verse in an envelope addressed 'to all my loved ones'. The BBC was subsquently deluged with requests for copies. My grandfather was an Ulsterman whose immediate family did not remain untouched by the Troubles.

Bibliography

Anderson, William, *Holy Places of the British Isles: A Guide to the Legendary and Sacred Sites*, London, Ebury Press, 1983.

Bates, Brian, *The Real Middle-Earth: Magic and Mystery in the Dark Ages*, London, Pan Macmillan Ltd, 2003.

Bates, Stephen, *A Church at War: Anglicans and Homosexuality*, London, I. B. Tauris & Co Ltd, 2004.

Beattie, Tina, 'Beauty back on camera', London, *Tablet*, 26 February 2000.

Benson, Peter, *The Levels*, London, Constable, 1987.

Blaikie, Thomas (ed.), *Victorian Love Poetry*, London, Macmillan, 1985.

Bowker, John, *The Meanings of Death*, Cambridge, CUP, 1992.

Bucknell, Barbara J., *Ursula K. Le Guin*, New York, Frederick Ungar, 1981.

Bunting, Madeleine, *Willing Slaves: How the Overwork Culture is Ruling our Lives*, London, HarperCollins, 2004.

'Reasons to be cheerless', London, *Guardian*, 1 March 2004.

Burns, Christopher, *The Condition of Ice*, London, Secker & Warburg Ltd, 1990.

Clack, Beverley and Clack, Brian R., *The Philosophy of Religion: A Critical Introduction*, Cambridge, Polity, 2000.

Davidson, Robyn, *Tracks*, London, Granada Publishing Ltd, 1982.

Davis, Charles, *Soft Bodies in a Hard World: Spirituality for the Vulnerable*, Toronto, Anglican Book Centre, 1987.

Dawkins, Richard, *The Blind Watchmaker*, Harlow, Longman, 1986.

Diski, Jenny, *Stranger on a Train*, London, Virago Press, 2002.

Doel, Fran and Doel, Geoff, *The Green Man in Britain*, Stroud, Tempus Publishing Ltd, 2001.

Faulks, Sebastian, *Birdsong*, London, Random House, 1994.

Garner, Alan, *Thursbitch*, London, Harvill Press, 2003.

Gee, Maggie, *Light Years*, London, Faber, 1985.

Gibran, Kahlil, *The Prophet*, New York, Random House Inc, 1999.

Greene, Barbara and Gollancz, Victor (eds.), *God of a Hundred Names: Prayers of Many Peoples and Creeds*, London, Victor Gollancz Ltd, 1962.

Heelas, Paul, *The New Age Movement: Religion, Culture and Society in the Age of Postmodernity*, Oxford, Blackwell, 1996.

Heelas, Paul and Woodhead, Linda, *The Spiritual Revolution: Why Religion is Giving Way to Spirituality*, Oxford, Blackwell, 2004.

Henshaw, Mark, *Out of the Line of Fire*, London, Sphere Books, 1990.

Hick, John, *Evil and the God of Love*, Basingstoke, Palgrave Macmillan, 1986.

Hutton, Will, 'Heed not the fanatics', London, *Observer*, 11 April 2004.

Jacques, Martin, 'A season in paradise', London, *Guardian Weekend*, 30 November 2002.

Jones, James, *The Thin Red Line*, London, Hodder & Stoughton, 1998.

Kundera, Milan, *The Unbearable Lightness of Being*, trans. Michael Henry Heim, London, Faber, 1984.

Le Guin, Ursula K., *City of Illusions*, St Albans, Granada Publishing Ltd, 1973.
The Dispossessed, St Albans, Granada Publishing Ltd, 1975.
The Farthest Shore, London, Victor Gollancz, 1973.

Lowry, Malcolm, *October Ferry to Gabriola*, London, Penguin Books Ltd, 1979.
Under the Volcano, London, Penguin Books Ltd, 1962.

Lynch, Gordon, *After Religion: 'Generation X' and the Search for Meaning*, London, Darton, Longman & Todd Ltd, 2002.

McFague, Sallie, *Speaking in Parables: A Study in Metaphor and Theology*, London, SCM Press, 1975.
Metaphorical Theology: Models of God in Religious Language, London, SCM Press, 1983.

Macfarlane, Robert, *Mountains of the Mind: A History of a Fascination*, London, Granta Books, 2003.

Mantel, Hilary, *A Change of Climate*, London, Penguin Books, 1995.

Marar, Ziyad, *The Happiness Paradox*, London, Reaktion Books Ltd, 2003.

Michell, John, *Sacred England: Traveller's Guide to the Legends, Lore and Landscape of England's Sacred Places*, Glastonbury, Gothic Image Publications, 1996.

Mitchell, Stephen, *A Book of Psalms: Selected and Adapted from the Hebrew*, New York, HarperPerennial, 1994.

Murgatroyd, Sarah, *The Dig Tree: The Extraordinary Story of the Ill-Fated Burke and Wills 1860 Expedition*, London, Bloomsbury, 2003.

Northcott, Michael, *An Angel Directs the Storm: Apocalyptic Religion and American Empire*, London, I. B. Tauris & Co Ltd, 2004.

Paley, William, *Natural Theology – Or Evidences of the Existence and Attributes of the Deity Collected from the Appearances of Nature*, Charlottesville, Lincoln Rembrandt Publishers, 1986.

Patterson, Hannah (ed.), *The Cinema of Terrence Malick: Poetic Visions of America*, London, Wallflower Press, 2003.

Peck, M. Scott, *People of the Lie: The Hope for Healing Human Evil*, London, Arrow Books, 1990.

Poliakoff, Stephen, *Perfect Strangers*, London, Methuen, 2001.

Powys, John Cowper, *A Glastonbury Romance*, London, Pan Books Ltd, 1975.

Priest, Christopher, *A Dream of Wessex*, London, Sphere Books Ltd, 1987.
The Affirmation, London, Arrow Books Ltd, 1983.

Schama, Simon, *Landscape and Memory*, London, Fontana Press, 1996.

Tennyson, Alfred Lord, *A Choice of Verse*, ed. David Cecil, London, Faber, 1971.

Thubron, Colin, *Turning Back the Sun*, London, Penguin Books, 1992.
Falling, London, Penguin Books, 1990.

Tolkien, J. R. R., *The Lord of the Rings*, London, George Allen & Unwin, de luxe edition, 1969.

Tomlinson, Charles, *Annunciations*, Oxford, OUP, 1990.

Vidal, Gore, *Creation*, St Albans, Granada Publishing Ltd, 1982.

Webster, Alison, *Found Wanting: Women, Christianity and Sexuality*, London, Cassell, 1995.

White, Vernon, *Identity*, London, SCM Press, 2002.

Williams, Rowan, *Writing in the Dust: Reflections on 11th September and Its Aftermath*, London, Hodder & Stoughton, 2002.

Wolterstorff, Nicholas, *Lament for a Son*, London, SPCK, 1997.

Wright, Alex, *Why Bother with Theology?*, London, Darton, Longman & Todd Ltd, 2002.
'An ambiguous Utopia', *Political Theology* 5:2, Equinox Publishing Ltd, April 2004.

Young, Julian, *The Death of God and the Meaning of Life*, London, Routledge, 2003.

Index